WHAT COLOR IS THE SKY?

China As Seen Through the Eyes of
An American Teacher and His Chinese Students

By

Michael Siems

"The Joy is in the Journey."

Hazrat Inayat Khan

Artwork throughout the book is the original photography of the author. The front cover photo, however, was taken by the author's friend and fellow teacher, Mr. Chen, from a painting on a Taoist monastery wall. Many thanks to all of those who have journeyed with me in and outside of China, on the 'intranet' of cyberspace, and elsewhere. Many thanks, especially, to my editor, graphics and book designer, the poet, Erjan J. Slavin, with wishes for bright nights of moonwalking under the April moon in every month and time of the year. "May all beings be well; may all beings be happy. Peace. Peace. Peace."

ISBN 978-0-557-59642-3

DEDICATION

To all of my students:
May you all be successful in your lives.
May you all pass your many examinations.
May you all find out who you really are.
May you all help build,
"A beautiful world
filled with
beautiful human beings."

Jiuhuashan, 2010

Pearl Park, Bengbu City

WHAT COLOR IS THE SKY?

TABLE OF CONTENTS

Be love...

Bengbu City

In a Village Near Bengbu College

Putuoshan Island

Invasion

Imagine being in another world where all of the aliens looked different than you, spoke another language, and where everything was foreign to your usual experience. Would this place be the planet Xerkon? No, just the Middle Kingdom, China—a country not light years away, but only a few thousand miles from your home.

My stay in China was a roller coaster of states and emotions, ranging from wonderment to culture shock, to isolation, and to integration; but I never suspected how culturally different it would be. I must say that the Chinese people are the most friendly and kind people that I have met anywhere in the world. I was universally welcomed and honored. That being said, China is a challenge for any foreigner. Why? Well, let me count the ways.

Most people in the Anhui Province, where I taught English, had never seen a foreigner—let alone talked to one. So, wherever I went in public, I was met with stares—not just with stares, but with open-mouthed amazement. Then that was followed by the immediate pronouncement, *"laowai"* (pronounced as low•way), which means, literally, "old foreigner." It was like a scene out of the science fiction movie, *The Invasion of the Body Snatchers*, when the aliens would see a normal human, and start pointing and screaming to alert the other pod people. Needless to say, I am neither one of the pod people, (at least not the last time that I'd checked,) nor one of the Han people. As my students told me, "You foreigners have big noses and different colored hair and eyes."

Next, many times, people would gather around me wanting to talk, particularly because I was on a college campus, where people want to learn English. The conversation would go something like this. "Where are you from?" I would reply, "America." Then, they would say," I want to learn English, but my English is very poor." I would respond, "No, you speak English well." Then they would say, "No, it is just so-so." Then, I would again reassure them that they spoke very well. This was always the preliminary introduction to varied topics including: home city, food, and studies.

In many ways, it really was like being famous. It was very difficult to go anywhere without people wanting to engage me in one fashion or another. I've always tried to be gracious and to give them what they'd wanted, whether that was to speak English, meet an American, or just to talk about America. However, sometimes, this constant engagement would present problems, especially if I were tired after a day of teaching or if I were ill. Sometimes, these meetings with people would end with pictures taken with them on their cell phones, or occasionally with autographs.

These glimpses of fame would at times escalate into crowds of people staring, laughing, pointing, and talking to me. Once, eating lunch in the city center of Bengbu, a crowd of children from the local school had gathered outside of the window, and was so joyously laughing, and shouting "Hello" to me. They were joined by all of the employees of the restaurant and by other passers-by. I went outside, and gave the children some candy, and they scampered away happily after having seen a foreigner. Another time, a student tried to converse with me, as I was vigorously rowing on a rowing machine!

My promenades through campus were like a continuous welcoming procession, saying hello to all the babies with their mothers—"*Ni hao,*" greeting the students with wishes for a good day, and then being asked where I was going—or being met by the stares of any adult who had been working on the campus grounds. Groups of students would wait until I would pass and, once they were several feet behind, shout hello.

If I were riding my bicycle, groups of students whom I didn't know would all yell hello and wave. Sometimes, they would even stop me and ask me if they would be able to ride my bicycle, to which I would oblige.

I guess this all should have been reassuring to me in that I knew that I still had a big nose, different colored hair and eyes; but fame is ever a double-edged sword. I never was chased by paparazzi—at least not to my knowledge. And I think that when I returned to the West, I was still a *"meiguo ren,"* an American person, and not one of the pod people!

The Silk Road

My Silk Road to China was not a unilinear path, but rather a winding course with many caravanserais, detours, dead ends, and sand traps in the desert. My life had undergone dramatic changes in the years preceding my journey along my personal "Silk Road to China." These life passages included: my wife's death from cancer, leaving my long term position as a case manager with the county government, travels hither and thither around the globe, relocating to the Eastern United States and back again, and working again in the field of disabilities. A wise friend once said that, "You need to learn when to catch the next wave at its apex and not get washed away in the trough." I was looking for that wave.

The historical Silk Road is a four thousand mile highway, with a northern and southern route that runs from modern day Xi'an in China and as far as Istanbul, Turkey. The Silk Road began sometime in China's Han Dynasty between 206 BCE and 220 CE. Winding through deserts, over mountains, along rivers, and across plains, the route linked East and West to transport slaves, silk, satin, musk, perfumes, spices, medicines, and jewels between empires. It also facilitated the spread of knowledge, religion, ideas, and even disease across great distances. Buddhism spread via the Silk Road from India to China. Although the popular image is one of a caravan marching along the entire route, the actual trade was accomplished by a series of traders, and not in a single journey (*Wikipedia*).

Similarly, my progress along the road to China was marked by starts and stops, engagements and disengagements. My life was shattered, when my wife of seventeen years was diagnosed with cancer. Our marriage was marked by a deep attachment to each other. We were literally "the sun and the moon" to each other. Our life in Southern Oregon was focused on living on our land in the nature, on our jobs, and our dogs. We had very few friends. When she died after three years of operations, treatments, and healings…I had to find a way to live without the person who was my foundation in life.

Consequently, I centered my life around my work, which was as a case manager providing services from the state of Oregon to people with developmental disabilities through the local county government. I loved my job, and I loved my coworkers, who in many ways were a surrogate family to me after my wife had died. I loved the camaraderie of working as a team to provide valuable services to a vulnerable group of people. I especially enjoyed meeting the families in our community and the sense that I was helping them receive services to help their children. As with any job, however…after seven years, which were at times very stressful, I decided that I needed time to rediscover my passion for life. I was propelled to make a change when the county government decided to privatize my department in a budget-saving maneuver.

After selling my house and six acres of land—which was in itself a very difficult decision—I began a three-year hegira to rediscover myself. I quit my job and began looking for the next wave. I had always wanted to travel, but like many other people, I had never had the time or the resources to pursue that dream. Now, with abandon, I began journeying to places that I had dreamed of since I was a child. India, Turkey, and China were the focus of my wanderlust; and I made several journeys to each of them. I became a different person: a citizen of the world.

I traveled to China twice during those years. My first trip was to Huangzhou, Huangshan, Tunxi, and Putuoshan Island. I was captivated by the modern skylines of the Chinese cities…and bedazzled by the echoes from its ancient history. I saw the beauty of nature, the dynamic growth, and the processes of modernization that characterizes China today. I loved the people with their friendliness and curiosity towards Westerners. My second journey along my personal Silk Road took me to Shanghai, Tai Shan, Qu Fu, Xibo, Qingdao, Penglai, and Beijing. I loved the caravanserai that was China.

Then, after more journeys, I decided to move from my beloved Oregon to the faraway land of North Carolina to be closer to some dear friends. While I was there, I made a very positive decision to take a several week course through Oxford Seminars to obtain TESL (Teaching English as a Second Language) certification. I had graduated from the University of Michigan years earlier with a B.A. and a teacher's certificate, so the coursework for the TESL was familiar to me.

For me the Oxford Seminar program proved to be a positive step towards finding a new profession and catching the next wave. The coursework included classroom management techniques, lesson planning, living and working abroad, teaching grammar, reading, writing, and information about finding teaching jobs abroad. The teacher was experienced, highly competent, and made the course very interesting. I was overjoyed to have received my TESL certification and a window onto my future.

Unfortunately, after a very short time, following the departure of some of my friends from the area, it was clear that I had made my way to a desert along a byway of the fabled Silk Road. Soon thereafter, I returned to Oregon to accept a job in my lifetime work in the field of disabilities. I did not feel that I was ready to begin seeking teaching jobs abroad.

After a year of working at this job, managing two residential programs for adults with disabilities, I had realized that I had just gone on another detour along that fabled highway, the Silk Road. I had returned to my lifelong field, only to find that I had grown and could no longer feel satisfied in that circumstance. I needed to find that next wave.

Sometimes in life, you find it hard to make a decision, and get stuck in the sand traps of the fabled road. I was in that situation, because I was attached to the beauty of Oregon, and found it difficult to think about going so far away to another country to teach—far from friends and family. I agonized for months over the dilemma; but in the end, the past propelled me to make a decision. I could simply not continue what I was doing and be happy. As a result, I initiated the Teacher Placement provision with Oxford Seminars.

Oxford Seminars helps graduates of their certification programs to find jobs in countries of the person's choice. I had asked them to help place me in a teaching position in either Taiwan or Turkey, feeling that Taiwan paid teachers well and that I had friends in Turkey. Unfortunately, I did not receive any immediate response to my résumé. So, I expanded my search to mainland China. I had misgivings about this, because I knew what living in China could be like, especially in the big cities…very different from Oregon!

I was immediately offered a position to teach English at a military college in a province in southern China. I agreed to the offer, even though I'd had reservations about teaching at a military college. Weeks went by, but I did not receive a contract or hear from the college. Finally, after contacting the recruiter, I found out that the province had just passed a law, prohibiting anyone older than fifty-nine years old from teaching, because a teacher had died at one of the colleges. I was amazed that they had not contacted me, but the recruiter told me that she would pursue positions for me with other colleges in other provinces.

Not long after, I received an offer from Bengbu City in Anhui Province to teach at Bengbu College. I had never heard of Bengbu, although I had traveled in Anhui Province a few years earlier. After some deliberation, I accepted the position to teach oral English, and embarked on a direct route along the Silk Road that led me to the Middle Kingdom.

The Clam Wharf

I only had a vague idea about the location of Chinese cities in relation to one another, and I began to search the Internet for information about Bengbu. Although there was not much information online, I had determined that Bengbu City was in the north central Anhui Province, or about 135 kilometers north of Nanjing, and 131 kilometers to the capital city of Hefei. I was pleased to see that Bengbu was at a 33-degree northern latitude, and I thought that it would be like the southern United States' climate, which was a mistake in my way of balancing, or assessing things geographically.

I'd read in *Wikipedia* that Bengbu means, "Clam Wharf," because it was famous for pearl production. Also, I'd learned that Bengbu was a small city by Chinese standards, with about three and a half million people in the general area. Bengbu was described as a small market town and port on the Huai River. It is an ancient town, which was first noted in the first millennium B.C.E. in myths surrounding the cultural hero, Emperor Yu.

It seemed exotic to be going to a town called "The Clam Wharf." I searched for information about Bengbu College, and found their website noting as a figure that it had nine thousand students. According to Bengbu maps, it was located on the outskirts of the city in an area known as the University District, where three universities converged. Along with Bengbu College, there would be Bengbu Medical College, which had many foreign students from Pakistan, and the Anhui University of Finance and Economics. This area is close to a large lake called Longzihu, or "Dragon Lake."

Historically, in 1948, it had been a major battleground in the Chinese Civil War, in which the communist People's Liberation Army defeated the Nationalist forces through the Huaihai Campaign.

Bengbu had been the center of water and land communications in the region for centuries. The city had also become well-known for food production, textiles, glass, chemicals, and electronics. Indeed, it was an industrial center for that part of Anhui Province.

I remembered my visit to the southern Anhui Province in 2005, when I visited Huangshan, the Yellow Mountain. It is a beautiful mountainous area, and in my mind I conjured up visions that Bengbu would be the same. I knew the beauty of the rural and agricultural areas of the province.

Wherever and whatever "The Clam Wharf" was, I knew that I was heading there. And I felt some peace that it was not a major metropolitan area, because my life had been rooted in a very rural part of Oregon. I didn't feel that the concrete cities that I had seen in China would be a great place for me to live in, and I prayed that Bengbu would be a better fit for me. At the same time, I was worried about the pollution that I had seen in some areas. I hoped that Bengbu would be more pristine.

The Three T's and the Big G

Over the course...of about a month, I had emailed and received emails from my contact in China, Derrick, regarding the particulars of employment with Bengbu College. Before being accepted as a teacher, I had a thirty-minute interview with two English teachers from the college. It was a standard interview, discussing my job history as a teacher, my interests, and possible ways that I would approach teaching the students at the college. It was a warm and cordial interaction, in which I was able to ask questions about the students: their English proficiency level, the size of the classes, and the course's materials. I was told that the students had a vocabulary of approximately one thousand words; that the class sizes varied, but were generally between forty to fifty students; and that there would be a text provided for the classes.

After my interview, I was faxed a form to take a physical with my local doctor that included an EKG, chest X-rays, blood work, and the normal battery of medical history questions.

Finally, it came in the mail—Chinese characters and addresses scrawled across the envelope...my contract to teach English at Bengbu College. It was with eagerness that I opened the mail to read the particulars of the document, which was to describe my future. In the context of other things being set aside, it was a formal contract requiring my signature; and after signing it with a calm sort of joy, I emailed it to my contact in China. The contract contained formal provisions for: salary, termination of the contract, prohibitions particularly in regards to proselytizing about religion, obeying China's laws, housing, medical services, reimbursement for air travel to and from China—and a statement on the maximum hours to be taught each week. Formally, an

English teacher in China is called a "foreign expert." I was certainly foreign, and I was hoping that I would be an expert in English!

Along with the contract, Bengbu College sent me the invitation letter, and some other documents that I had to send to the Chinese embassy in the United States in order to receive my "Z visa," which is the work visa for foreign experts to teach in the United States. This is essential documentation needed to teach in China.

My first concern was the monthly salary, which as stated in the contract, was to be 5000 RMB a month, which is approximately $700. I was not surprised by what, by Western standards, is a very poor salary to say the least. I immediately went online to determine if the salary was commensurate with what other teachers made in China. I was reassured when I determined that most foreign teachers made a base salary ranging from 5000-6000 RMB a month. This has to be measured by the fact that the cost of living in China is not very much compared with Western countries, and that 5000 RMB a month is a fortune in the Chinese economy, although it is not much by Western economic standards. I had later found out through my students that some teachers, who were teaching in the elementary schools, had started out in their teaching positions by making only 2000 RMB a month!

In addition to the salary, as a teacher at the college, I would have a free apartment with all utilities paid each month, except for my Internet service. Basic medical services were also included as a part of the contract. With these perks, a foreign teacher can live like a royal dignitary in the Chinese economy. Although the money saved by a foreign teacher in mainland China is not as great as in countries like South Korea and Taiwan, it is more than possible to save money as an English teacher.

The contract also stipulated that, upon meeting certain requirements, I would be reimbursed by the college for airfare, to and from China. This is no small concern for a teacher, because flying from the West Coast of the United States can cost as much as $1,000.

Another provision in the contract that is very important to a teacher is the number of hours in the classroom per week. My contract stipulated that I would be in the classroom for a maximum of eighteen hours per week. Also, I would be required to attend extracurricular activities with the students as deemed necessary by the college. This was to include the weekly English Corner, where students from all college departments gathered to discuss various topics in English, and to improve upon their learning of the English language in a general way. The number of hours that are required to be taught in the classroom is critical in deciding what teaching job to accept, because in some countries a teacher can be required to be in the classroom for up to forty hours a week!

The contract stated that either party to the contract could terminate the contract with a notification of thirty days. This was with the caveat that, if the teacher had desired to terminate the contract, he or she would then be required to pay from $800-$3,000 for a premature termination of the contract. This is a significant provision for prospective teachers to consider because I had found out, by doing research prior to my employment, that 75% of English teachers in mainland China do not complete their contracts! After my experience of teaching English in China, I was able to understand why it is so difficult to finish out a school year, but that is part of my story.

It is stated very clearly and in plain language in the contract that the teacher "will respect China's religious policies, and shall not conduct any religious activities incompatible with his/her status as a foreign expert."

The Chinese government is emphatic on the point that English teachers do not engage in proselytizing. The Big G, God, is clearly not a part of the Chinese educational system. During my first interview with Derrick, my contact there and the foreign affairs officer for Bengbu College, he told me that I was not to discuss religion or politics in the classroom. He said that the students could discuss religious and political issues, but that I was not to offer my opinion on these matters. And that brings us to the Three T's, which are the taboo topics in Chinese political life.

On my first trip to China in 2005, I learned about the Three T's: Taiwan, Tibet, and Tiananmen Square. These are the three forbidden topics in Chinese society, which cause significant political controversy. Taiwan is the island nation off the Chinese coast founded by the Nationalist Chinese and their leader, Chaing Kai Shek after their defeat by the Communist Army. Tibet is the former independent country situated in the Himalayan Mountains that was invaded and occupied by the Chinese in 1950. Tiananmen Square is the central square in Beijing near the Forbidden City, which was at the center of the pro-democracy student demonstrations in 1989 that had resulted in the massacre of numerous students by the Chinese Army. It was quite clear to me that as a foreign expert—an English teacher—I had to navigate my way around these issues and not to discuss them with the students in the classroom.

I had heard horror stories from other English teachers in China about college administrations not honoring the terms that were stated in their contracts. As it says on the United States Secretary of State website, "While many Americans have enjoyed their teaching experience in China, others have encountered significant problems. Some teachers travel to China with promises of a good salary, bonuses, and other amenities, only to find themselves in tentative situations, often lacking funds to return to the United States. You should verify the terms and conditions of employment with your school before accepting a teaching position in China." I am pleased to say that Bengbu College followed my contract to the letter. Salary was always paid promptly. I was honored as a professional by the college, and they strictly adhered to the contract and the agreement that I had made with them.

The next stage of my "Silk Road to China" was coming to even grips with the preparations that I would need to make for spending a year abroad. I was ready for my big adventure.

Kembay!

I was seated in an upscale restaurant in Bengbu while at a dinner to welcome me to the college, with the English faculty and the Bengbu College officials—including the president of the college, who in China was the head of the municipal Communist Party. There were about twenty people seated at various diameters around a lazy Susan that was covered with dozens of dishes representative of Anhui cuisine. Prior to the dinner, I was introduced to everyone, but significantly without their titles. As the honored guest, I was seated next to the college president, Mr. Wang, and another college administration official, Mr. Wu, whom I had later determined to be the administrative head of the English language department. Also, at the table were my two contact teachers, Mr. Wong and Ms. Zhou, and my foreign affairs contact, Derrick.

I immediately liked Mr. Wang, who exuded a power that only comes from being in political positions that make important decisions about people's lives. Everyone referred to him as "Number One." As we shared details about our lives and our travels, Mr. Wang would lift his glass filled with a "white lightning" liquor, and present toasts to the assemblage in a motion of welcoming their new "foreign expert" while shouting, "Kembay!" This enthusiasm would immediately be repeated by numberless other toasts of "Kembay" from the other people around the table. For me, a teetotaler, this was like the 2008 Beijing Olympics, but only it was a drinking competition in which I was unlikely to win the Gold Medal. "Kembay! Kembay!" We were cheering for the competitors. I really enjoyed the wide assortment of spicy dishes, which is typical of Anhui Cuisine, but I was soon awash in an alcoholic dream of Olympic proportions. Two hours later, we exited the restaurant, with everyone cheered by the Bengbu evening…while personally, I just tried to steer my body around obstacles, and to continue to put on the show of a modicum of sobriety, after my Olympic exertions.

My arrival in China had been preceded by months of preparation, both on the mental and physical levels, to move to a place on the other side of the globe. The importance of this preparation is so critical to the future success of living abroad. What to take and what to put into storage? Or quite simply, what needed to be *decided* to be done in preparation? List upon list of things to do needed to be checked off before my departure.

In many ways, the mental preparation can be a formidable antagonist in the drama of considering whether to live abroad. For me, it was the projection of what it would be like to live in China, based on the information from my two trips to the Middle Kingdom. I knew that, in many places, it meant living in large cities without the familiar comfort of forests, the moon, and the stars that I had been so well acquainted with in my Oregon home. Then, there was the foreknowledge of the pollution, which one encounters in parts and places around some of the industrial areas in China. Leaving Oregon for a year was in no small way like a death, because I knew how much I would miss Nature, my beloved Nature.

Also, I faced the significant realization that I would not see my friends and much of my family for a long time. This separation can be the most significant hurdle for an expatriate to face while living abroad, and I might suggest…the cross upon which many foreign teachers are crucified. It is very difficult to live away from the people whom you love for such an extended time. This too is like a death—the separation from the ones you love.

And so I did what I could to prepare myself for my journey: ending the lease on the house rental, stopping all bills for utilities, leaving a forwarding address at the post office, putting belongings into storage with friends, and deciding which things I would need for a year in China. Most importantly, I tried to gather medical supplies that I would need in case I became ill in the Middle Kingdom; but unfortunately, I forgot the most important item, the traveler's friend, anti-diarrheal medication.

It was difficult to try to pack my two allotted suitcases with everything that I would need for a year. Deciding which clothes I would need for both warm and cold weather was a major priority. Then there were all the books, the English as a Second Language books in particular, that I would need to teach at the college. In addition, I had worked for months, downloading lesson plans and other information that I would need for lesson plans in the classroom. So, it was with trepidation that I would be going to the airport in the hopes of weighing my luggage in and trying to make it with enough and not with more than that.

Then, began the farewell parties with friends in Oregon. Saying farewell to loved ones, and planning how to stay in touch, became the final acts in my preparations to leave for China. With some friends, I sensed a feeling that I was almost betraying them in leaving for so long, and with others there was a joyous acknowledgement that this was my future. What a delicate, and sometimes bittersweet tension parting is in our lives. Just to have the courage to leave loved ones is a big part of the journey.

The day finally came that I went to Portland to board my flight to Detroit, and to say goodbye to my parents. I wondered to myself when I would see Oregon again. Although the days I spent in Detroit were pleasant, because my parents are elderly (my father and mother are both in their mid to late eighties), there was the sense that we might never see each other again. China is a long way from Michigan, not to mention the distance between life and death.

Next, I flew to Istanbul to say goodbye to my friends in Turkey before the eventual departure for Shanghai. My stay in Istanbul was a pleasant interlude, and a preparation for my stay in a foreign land. As always, my journey was full of adventure—lost luggage, no clothes to wear—and then, enjoying the exotic place that is Istanbul. The day finally came for my flight to Shanghai and the start of my new life.

When I arrived in Shanghai, I was met outside the gates by four people from Bengbu College who had come to the airport to welcome me to China: Derrick, the foreign affairs officer from the college, Mr. Wong, a contact teacher, another man who was an administrator from the college, and the driver. There was a steamy August China heat that had also greeted me outside the airport. Everyone in my escort was so friendly and genuinely glad to see me. I was happy to find out that our van had air-conditioning for our six-hour drive to Bengbu.

As we drove through the metropolis of Shanghai in the stop and go of rush hour, I was impressed by just how big Shanghai is—it goes on forever, and it took us more than an hour to reach the outskirts of the city. I was so happy to meet my new friends from the college, and as we drove west toward Bengbu, I chatted with them about my life and asked questions about the college. They had brought many treats to snack on, including my favorite—moon pies—which is a pastry that the Chinese eat during the Mid-Autumn Festival that was due to occur in October.

Soon, sunset came and we continued our long drive to Bengbu. In the dark, we passed the former capital of Nanjing, the site of the Rape of Nanjing in *World War Two*, in which the Japanese massacred and raped hundreds of thousands of Chinese people. An hour later, we approached Bengbu, and I began to notice that the streets were filled with people on the hot China night. The streets were like a vision of what I imagined China to be. Orange Chinese lanterns glowed in the dark; people sat in groups outside of the restaurants talking or playing games; and dogs, chickens and cats patrolled the city on their nightly business. I could see that Bengbu was bustling with life—having not just a modern area with skyscrapers, but also having the picturesque mélange of Old China.

We stopped in the city to have a midnight feast at the *Champs d'Elysées*, a Bengbu restaurant, which used to be a theatre, but that had been turned into a French-themed restaurant. I thought to myself… "What an exotic way to start my adventure in China." Indeed, all of my fantasies about Chinese restaurants were soon fulfilled as dish upon spicy dish whirled around on the lazy Susan in front of me. I was famished after the long journey, and very appreciative of the dinner and the atmosphere of France transported to Bengbu!

Soon, we were on our way to Bengbu College, which is about a half of an hour drive from the city center. I could see that Bengbu was a modern city too with the distinctive futuristic architecture of China: domes, spires, and globes atop many buildings. There is such a mystery in arriving at new places in the night, with everything being half-veiled in the darkness, and also offering partial glimpses of the face of what was to become my familiar home.

As we wheeled up to the north gate of Bengbu College, with the name of the college written in English and in Chinese characters on the wall, the guards readily opened the gates in welcome of their new 'foreign expert'. We drove through the streets of the college to the far side of the campus where the teacher's apartments were located, and pulled up in front of the six-story brick building, which was to become my home. We climbed the steps to the third floor, and unlocked the door to apartment number 302. Oh, how happy I was to see my beautiful apartment! My primary fear about living in China was that I would have to live in some substandard apartment complex! So, much to my joy, I found my apartment to be not only nice, but to be delightful in every way.

It had a large bedroom, a sizeable office, a living room, a dining room, a bathroom, a kitchen, and two balconies! The purple pastel colored furniture complemented the elegantly decorated apartment. My companions showed me how thoughtful the college had been in providing me with kitchen supplies and utensils, with bedding, and even with bathroom supplies. There was a washing machine, but no dryer, because most people dry their clothes over a large metal rack that is set into the ceiling on the balcony of their apartments. Most importantly, they showed me how to operate the air conditioners located in the office and the bedroom! As my new friends departed, and I closed the door, I whispered a silent prayer of thanksgiving on the recognition that at least I would be happy in my new home. Later, Derrick told me that the college president, Number One, had said that my apartment was better than his!

The next days were a whirlwind of activity with my advisor, Derrick, orienting me to my new life at the college. I was guided on a campus tour, given a card to get food at the dining hall, and shown where to get buses to go into the city. The glamour of a new place gave my first days a pleasant glow.

On the night of the big "Kembay" feast in Bengbu, Derrick and three college officials, including the college president, Number One, came to my apartment to bring house warming gifts. One of the men took pictures of the new "foreign expert" talking with Number One. I realized then that my job as an English teacher was not only an educational position, but also had a significant political place in the chemistry that is the modern Chinese college. My teaching position—as with that of all foreign teachers in China—is part of the modernization of China…and China is very serious about entering the modern world as an English-speaking partner. I learned that it is critical to the Chinese communist system that graduates be able to speak fluent English. And as a component of that system, foreign teachers have an important role to play. I felt honored, and in a humble way, happy to be a part of that vision.

The Shire

When I first arrived, I would go into Bengbu by bus to go shopping or to walk around the park. Then, I would return via cab to the campus. A problem always came up when I tried to communicate to the taxi cab driver where I wanted to go. I knew that, in Mandarin, Bengbu College was pronounced something like "Bengbu Shir," but each time I would make my pronouncement, the cab driver would just stare at me in bewilderment. Then I would become resigned to pulling out the paper on which was written in Chinese characters the name, Bengbu College. Because "Bengbu Shir" sounded so suspiciously like "Shire," I started calling the college area, the Shire. Although I really was supposed to be in the Middle Kingdom, it sometimes felt more like Middle Earth to me—a charmed place with magic as its modus operandi. Although not peopled by hobbits or by other denizens of Middle Earth, I certainly felt like I was somewhere far away from my ordinary reality—hence, the euphemism of the place as, "The Shire."

The information that I had received in America about Bengbu College described a physical area of 247,000 square meters, replete with teaching buildings, a library, eight dormitories (four for each sex), an administration building, and a recently constructed gymnasium. The introduction also stated that there were nine thousand students and 408 full-time teachers and professors. The students, I later determined, were primarily from the cities and rural areas of Anhui Province, although there was a smattering of students from all over China, including a few from as far away as Tibet. In 2002, several colleges originally formed in the 1970's, were amalgamated to form Bengbu College under the direction of the Bengbu Municipal Government and the Anhui Education Commission. Bachelor's degrees were awarded to students in 46 disciplines, including Mechanical and Electronic Engineering, Food

Engineering, Arts Design, Computer Science and Technology, Economics and Management, Foreign Languages, Science, Music, Education, Physical Education, Arts Education, and Vocational Education. This was all embedded in the university, along with the two other universities in the area—and the Longzihu Center, a shopping area of restaurants, fruit vendors, and stores that served the over thirty thousand students from all of the universities.

Within the area that I called the Shire were also two small villages of brick dwellings, South Village and Yellow Blossom Village to the east of the college. From my apartment window, I could see an area of vegetable gardens, cultivated by teachers from the college, and green rice fields extending to Lushan Mountain or to South Mountain, as I called it. I loved this view out of my office window, and came to regard its magic as my home in the Shire. I could also see a small creek, which flowed toward South Village where white herons would fly like confetti thrown across a green horizon.

During my orientation, Derrick, my advisor, had shown me the blue teaching buildings, especially Building C, where most of my classes were to be situated. The gymnasium, and another dormitory for students, had just been completed—and the area surrounding them was not landscaped, with pieces of brick and other debris littering the area around them. It was like being at the center of a vast urban renewal project, with the detritus of the old still littering the new. The whole campus had the feeling of just being bulldozed, and small trees were now growing and beginning to start afresh. The other university campuses were beautifully landscaped, having been established for years, but Bengbu College was newer and had less money. Several months later, many magnolia trees and bushes were planted around these buildings to give them a pleasing appearance.

I was also surprised that, when I was shown the classroom buildings and the administration building, the floors were not as polished as would be the case in an American university, but rather looked like they had never been cleaned. I was to learn that this was standard practice in the classrooms, which often looked like they had just hosted the Woodstock Music Festival, with papers and other debris thrown on the floors by the students. This was a shock to my American sensitivity to cleanliness, and for me, order.

Most of the apartments in the two rows of teachers' buildings were empty. There was only one other apartment in my building, out of twelve apartments, which was occupied by another teacher and his family. So, there was a feeling of isolation and seclusion to my dwelling that I liked. On the other hand, it seemed like this area was always under construction, and with new apartments always being completed: drilling, pounding, and construction would go on day and night.

When I would walk the short few city blocks to the Longzihu Shopping area, I would be assaulted by the sights and sounds of thousands of students shopping, mostly in groups, for the necessities of their college lives. However, this was not like an American shopping center, but was truly Chinese. In the shopping area, the streets were filled with garbage and papers, and were quite literally filthy by American standards; but I loved its colorful atmosphere. All of the restaurants were always thronged with students. Popular Chinese music would be blaring from loud speakers placed outside of hair salons, pulsing with the throngs. Street vendors, with their wagons, would be selling exotic shish kebabs, or egg wraps from their stalls. It seemed that you could find anything that a student could desire in the stores, ranging from computer supplies, fruit, clothes, shoes, and bedding. It was always joyous and filled with the pulse and ever-changing energy of student life!

These halcyon days of initial surprise and wonder at my new environment were also days of preparation for living and teaching at the college. I wanted my apartment to be a haven, and a place of peace away from the atmosphere of the college. I was able to locate "plant street," where there were many shops that sold plants for people's homes. The Chinese people love beauty and always have green plants in their homes. Consequently, I was able to buy several large plants to make my apartment an American Eden, because they were so inexpensive.

Also, at the same time, one of the contact teachers, Ms. Zhao, took me to a friend's bike shop in Bengbu, where I purchased a flashy red mountain bike on which to ride around campus. I loved to ride around campus and the two villages greeting everyone with *"Ni hao"* and smiles. At night, especially on hot Anhui nights, I would ride around the campus in the dark, and listen to the popular music that the students played on speakers located everywhere on campus. I loved the sheer exoticism of being in a foreign place.

The Shire greeted me everywhere I went. People would shout hello, or wait because of their wonder at seeing a foreigner, and then say hello after I had passed by. Everyone would say *"laowai"* and sometimes point. Being in China, was initially a phantasmagoria of sights, sounds, and impressions that welcomed me every day!

Ni How???

During my stay in China, I would always greet a person with *"Ni hao,"* which is Mandarin for hello. I would also try to say, *"Xiexie,"* thank you, after most transactions. Quite often the Chinese person I was addressing would laugh or titter to those around them as if saying, "This *laowai* can speak Mandarin," or sometimes, I felt like they were saying, "Isn't it amazing that this barbarian can speak Mandarin?"

Before leaving for China, I had gone to the library and checked out CD's from the Pimsleur Language System so as to have at least a basic knowledge of the Mandarin language, the language spoken by most people in mainland China. I would drive around in my car for hours, trying to repeat the phrases, so that I would be able to talk to people. Although it was very difficult for me to produce some of the sounds that are so foreign to Western tongues, I thought that I had at least had a foundation for the beginning of my study of Mandarin. I was able to ask common questions, say hello, count, and to use simple phrases. I was confident that I was on the right track.

The Mandarin language, which is the *lingua franca* of China is also known as "Putonghua," the common tongue or the common speech of modern man. Even though different dialects are spoken in various areas of China, which are mutually unintelligible, Mandarin serves as the language that everyone can understand. The exception of course, would be that of a *"meiguo ren,"* an American person, or of any *"laowai"* from some other Western country who might have problems with most foreign languages.

Mandarin has two dozens of consonants and half of a dozen vowels, but what makes it one of the most difficult languages to learn in the world is the fact that it is a tonal language with four tones. This means that, upon any given verbal performance or "speech act," a basic word in Mandarin can mean several things depending on the tone used: whether it is uttered with a rising tone, say, or with a falling tone. So, a *"laowai"* like me could think that they were saying 'soup,' when really they were talking about someone's mother-in-law. On the day that I had learned this, standing in the dining hall of Bengbu College, I knew that I was really in trouble.

When I had first arrived on the campus, I had a general plan to learn Mandarin, at least in a rudimentary fashion. I had figured that I would find someone who'd wanted to learn English and would exchange my precious knowledge for the key to speaking Mandarin. Indeed, in my first days there, several people came to me with that intention. One man, who was a dormitory supervisor for one of the men's dormitories, would greet me each morning, and we became friends. He expressed his interest in learning English, and said that he would teach me Chinese. Unfortunately, I am ashamed to say, when I had learned just how difficult Mandarin was to speak, I decided to focus my energy on teaching and on meeting students. I believed that I knew the basics and "could get by."

I did try for quite a time to converse with people I would meet. I would go to the local Buddhist temple and try to talk to my friends there in my limited Mandarin; but one day a student went with me and was able to translate for me. He told me that the people at the temple did not understand a word that I had said!! They would simply stare at me when I tried to converse in Mandarin.

However, during my time in Bengbu, I could function with basic greetings. I could go to the market and ask for fruit, for example—giving the number I wanted in Mandarin—and then ask for their total price. Sometimes, I had difficulty in understanding what the vendor would say that an item had cost, but I was able to get by with my limited knowledge.

What makes living in China difficult is not only the spoken language, but also the written language, which is in Chinese characters, and not in letters like A-Z. A Chinese or Han character is a logogram used in writing Chinese. According to the article on Chinese characters from *Wikipedia*, there are over 47,035 characters, but, for most people, literacy is only the knowledge of 3,000-4,000 characters. These characters are 'morpho-syllabic': each corresponds to a spoken syllable with a basic meaning. "A majority of words require two or more characters to write." They are polysyllabic, but are distinct from the spoken syllables, and are dependent on the context of their characters for their meaning. Contrary to common knowledge, most Chinese characters are not pictograms, but are rather phono-semantic compounds.

If this sounds arcane, well, imagine a world in which most of the signs that you may see flashing in the night are some hieroglyphics from an alien tongue! To my eye, the Chinese characters are very beautiful. Walking in a typical shopping district in China is like seeing a world of indescribable beauty. That being said, you can't just read what the sign is saying, because you do not know any of the characters. So, when you are trying to find your way in a Chinese city, it is not necessarily a matter of reading signs because you may know some of the spoken language. I did not know any of the written characters!! This problem can extend to such a length that you might very rarely understand what a given item could be in a grocery store, because you cannot read what it says on the package. And sometimes, you can't tell what a thing is because you have never seen anything like it in America. It is a baffling world of foreign mystery.

It is true, however, that the Chinese have made a great effort to provide English language signs everywhere. So, many shops will have English signs with their name on them so that you can understand what they are selling. In most freeway systems in China, the signs are written both in Chinese and in English, although the directions given on them might not necessarily make sense to a Westerner.

Some examples of signs that I saw in China might give an idea of the humorous content and mistranslation common in China. For instance, I was eating in a hotel restaurant in the Anhui Province, and the waitress brought me the menu written in English. Some of the "delicious" items mentioned were: "pockmarked grandma's tofu," and "two headed fish eaten both ways." The most hilarious examples of the misuse of English in China could be found in the national parks. I laughed hysterically at a sign on a waste receptacle stating, "Fling trash here." Or another near a pond, "Careful drowning." Near one park, in a grassy area, the sign said, "I am small ordinary grass. Please leave green behind your footmark." My favorite sign, however, was on Putuoshan Island at a bathing beach, which proclaimed "Kind Notes." Among the Kind Notes were the following: "Take a medical checkup the first time you swim, doctor will tell you whether you are suitable to swim or not"; and "Let yourself calm in the open swim area, don't participate in swim competition, diving, or breath hold." After that kind note, I was afraid to put my big toe in the East China Sea. Yes, I was a *"laowai"* and a *"meiguo ren"* lost in the Middle Kingdom—truly, an innocent abroad!

Good Morning China!

Each morning would begin at sunrise with the neighbor hacking up phlegm from his lungs to start the day. This is a phenomenon that many men in China do to start the day, which is supposed to be health giving. It sounds exactly like they are going to expectorate pieces of their lungs! A wonderful way to get up…

Then I would hear the tractors coming down the roads from the villages, with their unmuffled engines echoing around the city…as though my life, freshly roused from dreaming and confused by the transition into the day, were visited by a vision of the combustion engines from hell. Unlike any vehicles elsewhere in the world, these machines, with their engines mounted on the front and often with a wagon affixed to the back, were like some throwback from the early Communist era. I could envision them working on the Maoist collective farms decades ago.

Then, my neighbor's alarm would sound two apartments above me. Although the alarm was not an unpleasant melody, the tune would play sometimes over and over for an hour, before they would shut it off and get out of bed. Sometimes, two alarms would sound with their distinctive melodies. I would walk around hearing the recurrent song in my head.

Next, the neighbor next to me would lock his husky dog on the front porch of his apartment, which would lead to a concert of howling that would go on for hours. This had started when the dog was a puppy and had continued for all of the months that I'd lived at the college. To my knowledge, no one had ever said anything about it, because the dog's symphony was a permanent feature of life in our apartments. In America, such prolonged howling would bring an immediate response from the police, who would be called by an irate neighbor.

Then, the neighbors would get on their motorcycles, whose alarms would go off so as to assure that anyone who had not been awakened by their dog would surely know that they were leaving for the school with their child. Sometimes, this would be a prelude to all of the older Chinese women, who would be outside, screaming at each other from apartment to apartment.

Down below, behind the apartment building, were the gardens that the families of the teachers tended. As soon as it was light, many elderly people would be in the gardens digging and watering the plants. Of course, this was accompanied by loud talking between the gardeners, so as to alert the neighbors that the sun had come up.

Construction-site China would be the next movement of the symphony with banging, drilling, and hammering coming from every direction, which always made me wonder what they were doing so early in the morning. However, I knew that modernization must go on, and that soothed my questioning mind.

The moment of the finale, the final and deciding movement in this grand cacophony of sound would come from the loud speakers that were affixed to all of the lamp poles around the campus. The morning student radio program would boom across the campus, playing a variety of music from either Chinese or American pop. Good Morning, China!

Angels

I was in a classroom with about forty Chinese students, consisting of predominantly young women—my first day as a foreign English language teacher, a day in early September, 2009. I was attempting to get the computer started so that I could begin my presentation, and the introduction of telling the students who I was and where I lived in the United States. However, I could not get the computer started, because I could not read the software on the opening page, which was in Chinese. I asked the students to come help me get the computer started…no response. I asked them again…No one moved from their seats, and they just stared at me as if I were speaking Swahili. I repeated my request—no response. Finally, after much trial and error, I was able to boot the computer up and get it started.

My teaching style is largely interactive: I ask questions to get the students to think, speak in English, and interact with each other. So, I began the first class by showing pictures of the beauty of my home in Oregon, and asking the students what they thought about the pictures. As I would say something to them in English, they would stand reluctantly, and stare at me as if the Swahili that I was speaking was getting more complex. Sometimes, a student would utter something in response to what I was saying, while still others had acted so stunned that they could not speak. Meanwhile, all of the students had turned their heads parallel to their desktops so that I could see only rows of black hair on top of their heads, and no faces. It was as if I had encountered a whole flock of ostriches, all with their heads stuck in holes! This was the level of interaction with all of my nine classes that week. I was stunned! How was I going to teach oral English to students who were so passive and catatonic that they were like the living dead?

Much later, I was told by one of the students who had befriended me that his fellow students were so frightened of me, when they had first met me, that they could not speak. He said that they had never met a foreigner before, and definitely had never spoken to one. They were terrified. Also, the students were probably taken aback by the rapidity of the American English that I had been speaking until I had learned to modulate my speech and to speak slower. Other students had told me that Chinese teachers usually just lecture or read from a text, and so, my teaching technique of asking questions was askew of the normal didactic approach of their teachers. This, combined with the natural tendency of the Chinese students to be modest and reticent about speaking in class, made my job as an oral English teacher into a mountainous challenge that could only be compared to climbing a cultural and linguistic Everest. I just was not sure what to do.

After the cold bath of these first classes, I went home and reflected upon the experience. I had to determine a way to get them to know that it was their turn to speak and to interact with me. Suddenly, I recollected how the Native Americans would sit around a council fire and pass a "talking stick," a stick, which when passed, gave the possessor of the stick the sole right to speak. That person was not to be interrupted until they had completed their discourse. I thought to myself: "What can I use as a talking stick?" Finally, I decided that I would just use a blue handkerchief, which had been knotted up, as my "talking stick."

So, at my next class, I started speaking to the assembled students in my proverbial Swahili, and told them about the usage of a talking stick, and explained that my talking stick was my blue handkerchief. So, when I threw my handkerchief to them that meant it was their turn to answer my question and to speak. They were shocked, when I lofted my handkerchief in the air, which then fell in one of the student's laps. Immediately, the effectiveness of the tactic became apparent. Even though I did not know their names, I could designate the speaker and compel him or her to stand and answer my questions. This became a fun game, when I would throw it from one end of the classroom to the other, occasionally hitting someone in the head, bringing a lot of laughter. My modus operandi had been born.

When I went to China, I knew very little about the Chinese educational system. Later, I learned that the Chinese educational system is a state-run system of public education. According to an article in *Wikipedia*, all citizens must attend school for at least nine years. "The government provides primary education for six years, starting at age six or seven, followed by six years of secondary education for ages twelve to eighteen." This is three years of middle school and then three years of high school. Students learn a foreign language, which is usually English, beginning in the third grade.

During the Cultural Revolution (1966-1976), the system of higher education in universities virtually ceased. However, after a renewed commitment by the government to higher education, by 2003, China supported 1,552 institutions of higher learning (colleges and universities), 725,000 professors and teachers, and eleven million students. *Wikipedia* cites that, "The percentage of China's college age population has increased from 1.4% in 1978 to roughly 20% in 2005." An extensive standardized exam system is the basis for selecting academically able students.

My students, all five hundred of them, which comprised all of the students in the English department, were by and large women, who made up ninety to ninety-five per cent of each class. They really were like angels to me: joyous, innocent, and emotionally immature for eighteen to twenty year olds. They reminded me of freshmen in an American high school more than of college students. They were always laughing, and members of the same sex were very physically affectionate with each other: holding hands, embracing, and literally sitting in each other's laps at times.

My Chinese students functioned as a group. Each class, which usually had between forty to fifty students, went to all of the same classes together, and rotated across campus from one class to the next together. Essentially, these same students in each class would remain together for the three to four years while they were students at Bengbu College. I learned later that this is a tenet of the Chinese educational system: that students should always be organized in groups, so that they can learn cooperative skills.

These classes of students functioned as a group in all classroom interactions. Each class had a classroom monitor who functioned as a liaison between the English department administration and the teacher. The monitor made announcements, kept roll in the classrooms, and followed my instructions as a teacher. This group consciousness extended even to classroom performance. If a student who had been asked a question did not know an answer or simply did not understand the English question, all of the students around him or her would give the answer in Chinese or English, or translate the question into Chinese so that the student could understand. As a teacher, it really was like interacting with one organism rather than with individual students.

These class groups even lived together in the dormitories. As previously mentioned, there were eight dormitories, four for each sex. Students lived in dormitory rooms with six students to a room. So literally, many of the students lived with their classmates for twenty-four hours a day, which caused deep bonds to develop between students. These students would live together for their whole college life. As a result, it was the norm to see two students of the same sex, walking hand in hand or arm in arm across campus. There were deep emotional bonds developed between students. Not only would you see two students together—but often, whole groups of students walking together across campus. I often pointed out this difference to my students: that in America, students function more often as individuals. I told them that if six American students had lived in the same dorm room, instead of the normal two students, it would be like the last act of a Shakespeare play, with not a student left standing.

Physical conditions in the dormitories are also very different than at American universities. There are no showers in the dorm rooms. Each evening you would see students carrying a large almost two-gallon thermos across campus to the bathroom where they would get hot water to bathe. This is a little inconvenience, when compared to the fact that the dorm rooms have no heat, but more about this later.

Because China has a very traditional culture, there is a very great segregation of the sexes. Not only are the men and women separated in different dormitories; but even in classes, there is an informal separation. The women sit together, and the men sit in another area of the classroom. While this is an informal grouping, and some men will sit with their girlfriends, it was readily apparent that the women did not sit with the men. This even extended to communication. The women most often only spoke with their friends around them, not to the few men in the classes. One student told me that even after three years of being with the same women classmates, he did not know all of their names! By and large, even on campus, men did not associate with the women students. Of course, there were many couples in romantic relationships, and you would see them walking arm in arm in secluded areas of the campus at night; but this was the exception to the rule of segregation. Unlike on American college campuses, there was very little dating or interaction between the sexes. Students told me that they were there to get an education, and this was paramount in their lives—not a relationship, which was to come only after graduation, when a job had been secured.

My students were mostly from poor families in the Anhui Province, and many were from farming families who grew rice for a living. During class, one student showed pictures of his home, and it looked exactly like the homes in the villages surrounding the campus—a small brick dwelling, with maybe one room. In American terms, it would be regarded as being extremely impoverished.

All of my students—regardless of what their background was—were eager to learn and were very serious students. I was always amazed by their innocence, their joy, and their indefatigable love for life.

The Washerwoman's Son

One of my teacher contacts, Ms. Zhao, and I were on the Bengbu to Hefei train, during rush hour, headed to the capital city of Anhui Province for a physical that I was told was a requirement for any foreigner working in Anhui. This was in addition to the physical that I had taken and paid for in the United States. The train was crowded with workers, who make the daily commute two and a half hours one way to work. Ms. Zhao and I chatted about our experiences as teachers. She told me about her life at the college, and what it was like to live in Bengbu.

When the train arrived in the Hefei area, I could see that Hefei was a significant metropolis with many high-rise apartments and industrial areas. It is a city of four million people, and has one of the largest freshwater lakes in China, Lake Chaohu. It seemed to take a long time, beginning from the outskirts of the city, to reach the city center and the train station. We then disembarked from the train, and took a taxi to the medical office.

There is an old story that the ultimate stage in surrender to things in life comes when you die and the washerwoman comes to clean your corpse in preparation for burial. At the medical office, during my physical, I was given a glimpse of what it is like to be the washerwoman's son…to be in full surrender. Medical clinics and hospitals in China are not like similar medical institutions in the West because there is little privacy. On one of my trips to China, I had a physical at a major hospital, and was surprised by this lack of privacy. For instance, a phlebotomy and normal blood draws were completed in a large public room, with a long line of people waiting together for the phlebotomist to do the blood draw in the full view of other patients. This experience was to be no different. We would go from room to room and station to station to complete the various parts of the examination: X-rays, chest examinations, blood draws, and other examinations. There would be large groups of men who would go one by one to be examined. As I had my x-ray completed, I had to take my shirt off in full view of other patients and Ms. Zhao, and then was pushed and positioned by the x-ray technician like I was just a piece of meat—it was forceful! I just laughed to myself and thought about the washerwoman, in all of her glory and in full control of my body. Fortunately, the doctors had determined that I had some life left in my body, and did not call in the real washerwoman.

After the examination, we had lunch in a pleasant restaurant and went to the bus station to return to Bengbu. I enjoyed the ride back on the bus because I was able to see that most of Anhui Province was very rural. Farms, rice fields, and villages one after the other dotted the whole distance to Bengbu. It was beautiful and I could imagine a rhythm of life that really had not changed for centuries.

The first month at Bengbu College was a September of heat, cultural adjustment, and the wonder of a new environment. I soon started a routine of classes four days a week, which kept me very busy. I would walk the five minutes from my apartment to the blue classroom building in the afternoon heat, and by the time I had reached the classrooms, my shirt would be soaked with sweat—and I would feel like I was going to faint. The temperatures were in the nineties with a similar humidity. Every day I would take two or three showers just to stay cool. Even at night, it would be very hot and humid, and I was so thankful for the air conditioning in my apartment.

I would ride my bicycle in the morning to explore the two nearby villages. One village, which I had called "Yellow Blossom Village," was to the east of the campus, and was garlanded with yellow squash vines covering most buildings and walls. The brick dwellings were humble, usually one-room houses, with little furnishing. But there was an air of dynamic life about the village: people were sitting in groups playing games or chatting; children were walking along the road returning from school; and people were washing clothes in large wash basins. Oxen stood tied to trees; chickens scratched about in the dirt; and dogs patrolled the village on some canine business. I could see that there were even some small industries in the village—women were working on sewing machines and there was a small foundry. Despite the poverty, there was a dynamic feeling of village life. I had to be careful, however, because of all of the cars and motorcycles that zoomed down the road, oblivious to pedestrian or to bike traffic.

The other village which I had dubbed, "South Village"—because it was south of campus—was smaller, and in some ways more rural than the other village. There were many rice fields surrounding the village. There were many gardens, and it seemed more agricultural than the other village. I enjoyed riding my bicycle there because there was less traffic, and I felt it was safer to ride my bicycle through the rice fields. Just outside of the village, there was a large brick factory, and a smokestack which belched smoke and produced the bricks which were stacked around the establishment. Outside of the village, I could see Longzihu Lake and, in the distance, the Bengbu skyline.

Eating in the college dining halls was also an exercise in surrender. There were two dining halls, each with three floors, where the students would eat. Imagine nine thousand students swarming around the front of the areas where the food orders would be taken for the dishes on the menu, which were either rice dishes or noodle dishes. Students told me that there is a division in what is eaten in China: in Northern China noodles are eaten, and in Southern China rice is eaten. Apparently, Bengbu is the dividing line between these two diets, and, therefore, both diets were served at the college. People were always asking me whether I preferred rice or noodles, because this was very important to their view of which cuisine I, or anyone perhaps, should like. For me, it was largely another proposition that awaited my surrender. I would look at what the students were eating, and point at the dish that I wanted. I had to eat what the students ordered. I was restricted to what I could see that other people were eating, and not to what was on the menu—because I could not read the menus that were in Chinese.

The other cultural difference that I noted immediately was that, as I stood by the counter to order my food, the students would not form a queue, but would stand in throngs pushing to the front of the counter. So, I would get sandwiched in by the students, who were literally standing so closely together that they were shoving me. As a Westerner, who is used to personal space, this was a challenge and I would immediately step back to gain more space around me. It took me many months to become more accepting of this lack of space. In China, there are so many people that, in most instances in public, there are no queues; people just shove their way forward.

Another space-related observation that I made was that the throngs of students walking from their dormitories to the lunch rooms or classes never stopped or hesitated if I happened to have been approaching from the opposite direction. In America, it is natural and polite to give way when another person approaches from the other direction, but not in China. People just keep going; and I kept thinking every day that there was going to be a major collision between this *laowai* and a student.

Sometimes, I would take the bus into the city center to shop or just to walk around the park. Riding the bus, jammed with students, we would bounce all the way into town; but who could complain? It was so inexpensive to ride a bus: only one yuan (about fourteen cents). As I sat on the bus, everyone would be staring at me; and, occasionally, some student would be courageous enough to ask me where I was from. Most of the time, I would just watch the amazing city sights glide by...vendors cooking Chinese meals on every street, fruit markets piled high with colorful fruit, people hurrying everywhere around town, chickens scratching on the sidewalk for a treat, and all of the businesses with their colorful signs in Chinese. It was a phantasmagoria of sights and sounds.

Usually, I would get off near Pearl Park, where the bus route ended, and walk from there through the park. The park was very beautiful with several gold-roofed pavilions, including one pavilion on an island in the lake. Many men would be gathered around playing games; some played Chinese musical instruments; groups of women would be practicing dance routines, and other people would be fishing in the lake. Parks in China are places where families gather on days off from work to stroll, and to enjoy the peace. In Pearl Park, there were even little paddleboats, each shaped as a different cartoon character, in which children would paddle around the lake. On sunny days, people in the surrounding apartment buildings would hang cages with birds outside their windows, and the park would resound with the melodies of their flutelike songs. For me, Pearl Park was a magical place where I could forget school, and just enjoy the beauty.

The other dizzying fact of life in Bengbu was the swirl of traffic. Conveyances of all kinds roamed the streets: bicycles, motorcycles, electric bikes, carts, cars, buses, and trucks. It was a challenge to cross any street because the laws were very different in China. Traffic would not stop at red lights if parts of it were making turns; and so, consequently, if you or a pedestrian were crossing at a crosswalk, you would have to watch at all ways to be sure that some vehicle did not hit you. They will not stop for a pedestrian, because seemingly, the vehicle has the right of way. They will run you over if you are not careful. Taxis and buses are particular adversaries for the pedestrian. Taxi drivers drive as fast as they can and will not stop for anything. Buses will come so close to your legs that you feel like the jet stream that they leave behind will take your leg off by itself. Once, I watched a very elderly couple trying to cross at a busy crosswalk with traffic coming from every direction. There was a traffic control officer waving the traffic along, but he made no attempt to stop the traffic flow or to aid the seniors as they cowered in the traffic that swirled around them. Somehow, they made it across the street and lived until the next time they tried a crossing. I found particularly the electric motor bikes to be a problem, because they would make no sound as they whizzed by you, and came up from behind at the speed of light. At the same time, most vehicles were using their horns to beep at each other, or at anything that might have come into their view—and by joining their various noise together—had created a cacophony of sound, which reached a decibel level of inconceivable proportions. For a foreigner, it is difficult to cross streets until you understand the traffic rules, and hopefully this happens before you are an assignment for the washerwoman.

On other days, I would walk past Pearl Park to the shopping district, where there were many vendors and shops selling clothes, shoes, and electronic goods. This area would be very crowded, usually, with women shopping. My goal, however, was an American Mecca—McDonald's, the only one in Bengbu. Yes, I must admit that I enjoyed going to the fast food paradise for a number of reasons, even if I would never go to one in America. The first time I walked in the door, the McDonald's employees looked at me like it was the Second Coming of Christ—a real American in McDonald's. I liked McDonald's in China for several reasons. I could get a large cup of pretty good coffee; I could eat something different from rice or noodles; and I could sit in an environment that reminded me moderately of home. Of course, I was stared at for the entire time that I would be in the restaurant, but it was just as refreshing to get that coffee buzz, and to taste that decadent hamburger and fries! Yes, I am a sinner. There were other more upscale coffee houses in Bengbu, which served espresso and other delights, but it was very expensive and the cups of coffee were small. Thank you McDonald's...for providing an oasis to a stranger in a strange land.

Sometimes, I would take the bus in to buy a few items at the only large grocery store in Bengbu, Carrefour. Carrefour is a huge store with household items and clothing on one floor, and food and grocery items on the second. Each time I went to the grocery section, I was in awe at the variety of both the fruits and meats, and also at that of every conceivable edible that could potentially be enumerated. The main challenge as a foreigner is that the packaging of the foods is very different in China, the lettering usually in Chinese; and sometimes, I just did not know what the food item was. I had my mission, however, and I would search out the imported foods section to buy my favorites: canned tuna fish, muesli, olives, pasta, and crackers. I really treasured the orange juice and the yogurt drink that I could buy at Carrefour. It was food heaven! On the other hand, it was a bizarre journey in Chinese cuisine because every part of an animal was eaten in China: head, snout, feet, and intestines. The works! Then I would see exotic things, like the green snakes that were put on display or the blackened ducks without feathers. While shopping, I was really in the hands of the washerwoman, because so much of the grocery store was incomprehensible to me.

After shopping at Carrefour, sometimes I would go to the other American Mecca in China, Kentucky Fried Chicken. Kentucky Fried Chicken is the most popular fast food emporium in China—the Chinese people love the Colonel! For me, just to have a chicken sandwich and some fries was a pleasurable experience, and was simply different from Chinese food. It made me happy to be there and have a treat. Thank you Colonel!

Then, after my shopping expedition, I would take a taxi back to the Shire, instead of lugging my loaded grocery bags on the bus. After I had learned that I was never going to properly pronounce, "Bengbu Shir" or whatever in Mandarin, I would simply whip out a paper with *that* written in Chinese characters, and like magic, be whisked off to the college within fifteen minutes. I always felt a level of satisfaction, when I reached into my pocket to pay the cab driver, and knew that I had successfully found my way in and through the city. Ah, but there was another problem.

Each time after paying him, I would give the taxi driver a tip; but, invariably, he would look offended and give it back to me. This happened several times before I had figured out that I was not supposed to tip the taxi driver. And then it happened...I was in the nicest coffee house in downtown Bengbu drinking a four-dollar cup of cappuccino, which was in a cup the size of a thimble; and I left a sizeable tip for the waitress, and headed out the door. I was a block down the street, when I saw the waitress running down the street towards me, waving the tip in her hand. I was shocked when she bowed and handed me the tip! Then I realized that you are not supposed to tip in mainland China. Yes, *laowai*s, you are not supposed to leave tips anywhere!

The inability to communicate on most levels would create a situation in which one would feel as though one had regressed to the level of an infant again, being dependent on others for many of the necessities of life. *Wah! Wah!*... You feel like a baby! I must admit that, by the end of the first month, some of the culture shock had worn off—and I was more docile in the hands of the proverbial washerwoman. I had truly surrendered to her loving hands, and to the vagaries that are the customs of Chinese culture. Oh, but there were more adventures still to come!

Ponytails and Machine Guns

The freshmen students did not arrive on the campus until the end of September, but it was apparent when they arrived, because giant red balloons floated back and forth in the sky over the main road into the college welcoming them. With the arrival of a few more thousand students, I was again greeted by the renewed calls of *laowai* and with stares of disbelief as the students became acclimated, now for the first time again, to a foreigner being on campus.

And then it happened. One September morning I went to the dining hall for breakfast and saw that all the new students, men and women, were dressed in blue and gray camouflaged military uniforms. This was a shock, because suddenly I felt like I was on an army base and not on a college campus. That morning, the students began drilling.

Regular officers from the People's Liberation Army began marching columns of students across the main square and roadways of the campus. The students would march back and forth shouting, "*Yi, er, yi…*" or "One, two, one," as their drill instructors educated them in the basics of marching. This was an amazing sight to me, because many of these students were young innocent-looking women, only eighteen years of age. It was difficult for my Western mind to comprehend these young women, with their ponytails flopping hither and yonder as they marched, shooting machine guns at an enemy: they didn't look like warriors to me. Of course, this perception was underscored by my perception of the students in my class who, as I have said, were so immature in many ways—being not even, really, young men and women. But the students were definitely into the spirit of the whole military thing, because I would see them practicing their marching in small groups without officers. I later learned that all college students upon entry to school must participate in fourteen days of military training.

In China, military service is compulsory at age eighteen for everyone, male and female. The People's Liberation Army is the world's largest army. With three million service people, 2.5 million people are on active duty status. As a result, the Bengbu College students were being trained to be future soldiers in the Chinese military. Other aspects of the Chinese military were evident in the skies over the college. On many days, during my stay in China, the military would conduct training flights over the campus with two modern-looking jets going back and forth for hours over our heads. The sound of the jets flying at a very low altitude was a constant distraction and disruption to life on campus. I had always thought to myself that such low level flights would never have been allowed in America because of the noise. You could hear the jets streaking overhead even in the classrooms.

When I first arrived in Bengbu, I took several bike rides into the downtown area and as we were riding, I would see all of these large buildings with fences surrounding them, and ominous-looking antennas and satellite dishes on top of the buildings. When I asked a student what they were, he said, "Oh, that is the secret police building." When I asked who they monitored, he said, "Criminals." I had the definite impression that everything was being monitored in Bengbu.

So, for fourteen days, the freshman students marched back and forth on campus shouting their cadences as loudly as they could. I would be in the classroom, trying to teach, and sometimes the sound would be so deafening that it was hard to hear the replies of the students in the classroom. And, with my American mind, I felt distinctly uncomfortable throughout the experience of seeing thousands of people walking around in military uniforms. I would also see the PLA officers strolling through campus. I felt more as though I were at West Point College in the United States than at Bengbu College in China.

Consorting with Communists

At the end of September, Derrick, my advisor, told me that there would be a dinner for all of the foreign experts from all over Anhui Province in Hefei. So, that week, Derrick and I went with a driver and another foreign teacher, whom we picked up at an elementary school where he taught in Bengbu. He was from Morocco, and we chatted for the two-hour drive to Hefei about teaching in China. He said that he taught beginning English to kindergarten students. He said that he really enjoyed teaching in China, and that it was not difficult to teach the young students who had not any knowledge of English. It was his second year in Bengbu, and he had his own apartment in the city where he lived with his Taiwanese girlfriend. He said that he was currently reading the novel, The English Patient, and we both exclaimed how wonderful the book was; and what a shame it was that Chinese college students could not read modern literature like that. It was a pleasant journey to Hefei, as we watched the beautiful countryside and the villages just outside of the window.

When we arrived at the five-star hotel in Hefei, I was so happy to see the green landscaped gardens with flowers all around the hotel. It was like being in Oregon again. There was even a small lake, directly in front of the hotel, where we strolled before dinner began. Then, we went inside to await the beginning of the affairs for the afternoon. I was surprised to find out that we were going to be given a tour of a research facility in the city; and we were soon ushered onto a bus with many other foreigners.

As the bus sat, waiting to depart, I introduced myself to the people sitting around me. Two were an Italian and a Swiss businessman living in Bengbu. That was when I realized that the dinner was not only for teachers, but also for any foreigners living in the province. As we had passed a large lake in an area that had a park-like setting, we arrived at the National Laboratory for Nuclear Fusion, a joint international research project with several nations involved, including the United States. The Topomak research center was a large facility, housing a reactor for nuclear fusion research. A scientist gave us a lecture about the project to develop nuclear fusion, and I was excited to hear about the project because, as he said, if nuclear fusion could become viable it would provide all of the energy that the planet would need without the hazardous waste. Nuclear fusion is similar to the way that stars, like the Sun, function in changing hydrogen into helium. I was particularly surprised as the scientist described the high temperatures generated in the reactor. We were then taken on a tour of the large reactor, which was situated in a room that was many stories tall. For me, this was a very interesting experience.

We then returned to the hotel where the banquet was about to begin. At the head table were the governor and the vice governor of the province, along with many other provincial government officials, and several foreign experts who were being honored with awards for their teaching. Prior to the dinner, groups of teachers from different colleges performed skits to entertain the assemblage. There were teachers from all over the world, including Germany, Africa, Canada, and Australia. It was then that I realized that the foreign experts in China were not all from English-speaking countries, but rather they were also from countries in which English was not the first spoken language.

The banquet itself was a sumptuous spread, with a buffet that was like that in the finest restaurants. Wine and other alcoholic beverages were served with the meal, and along with the formal speeches, we had many toasts. The governor of the province came to our table, and I, along with the other foreigners toasted our glasses with him. It was evident that this gathering was a very political affair covered by the newspapers. The teaching of

English in the universities and colleges of Anhui Province is part of the Chinese modernization of the country, and is critical to its success. This is central to the Communist party's political program. It suddenly came to me that my teaching English had played a significant role in the life of modern China. I felt honored to be a part of this, as I feel that the Chinese government is very smart to promote English in the educational system. In the future, if not now, many Chinese people will be able to speak fluent English, and so to conduct their business and international affairs. I was definitely consorting with Communists!

Several months later, I was astonished to find out that many of the administration officials and teachers at Bengbu College were members of the Communist Party. Whenever I would be introduced to people at the college, I was never really told who they were or their function in the college administration. One day, I took pictures with the different senior graduating classes, and I was seated in the front row with many teachers and officials. The woman who was seated next to me seemed very friendly, and we talked a little about my experiences at the college. Later, when I received a photo from that day, I asked the student who the people were. He said, "Oh, she is the Communist Party head of this department. And he is the head of the Communist Party for the English department." In my *naïvetè*, I had not realized that many of the teachers and administration officials were members of the Party. I asked the student if there were students who were members of the Communist Party. He told me that in his class there were approximately ten students who were Party members, and that Party members did enjoy benefits that other students did not have. He stated that he was sad that Chinese society was not equal, and that he had felt disadvantaged because other students had perks that he did not enjoy.

On the other hand, I went out to dinner once with two of the Chinese teachers from the English language department. As we were eating dinner, and discussing things in the context of our observations about life, they both pointedly told me that they "are not interested in politics. We just want to lead a happy life with our families." I thought to myself that that statement would have been shocking in China just a few decades ago. How things had changed!

My role as a foreign teacher at the college was certainly governed by the politics of modern China, and was distinctly a part of the modernization of Chinese society. The more I lived in China, the more I was to understand the depth to which the Communist Party and that ideology directed society.

Amithaba and the Huai People

In the month of September, a student and I rode our bicycles to the small Buddhist temple, "The Temple Beneath the Rock," which was about a twenty-minute ride from campus. It was always difficult to get there, because construction on the high-speed railway ran along the bike route. Once we had turned up a dirt road, which lead beyond a large quarry and a rocky hill, it was a much easier ride. Although in the country, the area had small factories, including a small foundry, which belched black smoke. I was enchanted, though, when I reached the temple area to see a Quan Yin statue in front of the new temple that was being built. We carried our bicycles into the inner compound, where construction on the temple was taking place. The new temple was going to be large and very beautiful when it was completed. We went around the new temple and into the old temple area.

Incense was burning and candles were lit in front of the temple. Two elderly women greeted us with a bow and the Buddhist greeting, "Amithaba." They were very friendly, and, of course, interested in where I was from. My student friend talked with them, while I went inside and did prostrations to the Amithaba statue within the temple. One of the women came over to me and demonstrated the correct prostrations, and associated motions, with my hands. I went into another room where I prayed before a small statue of Quan Yin, the feminine Buddha of Compassion. The two women told my friend that another foreigner had come the year before, and a monk from the temple had taught him the proper way to bow. After buying some incense, we left the temple. I was so happy to have found such a wonderful temple near my new home.

Buddhism has a long history in China, having come from India along the Silk Road, and was already well established during the time of the first emperor in 213

BCE (*Wikipedia*). Many foreigners came by the fabled Silk Road to teach and translate the sutras. In China, most Buddhists follow the Mahayana, of which the Pure Land sect is the major group. The Amithaba Buddha, The Buddha of Infinite Light, is the principal Buddha that is worshipped. Buddhism adapted itself to Chinese life by incorporating the traditional ideas of filial piety, ancestor worship, and the hierarchical system. In the Fifth Century C.E., the Buddhist saint, Bodhidharma, brought Chan Buddhism to China from India. Buddhism was the dominant religion in China until the Communist era, when during the Cultural Revolution many temples were destroyed, and monks were killed, and religion was repressed. However, in the last few decades, Buddhism has again resumed its prominent role in many Chinese peoples' lives.

We climbed the rocky hill behind the temple, and were greeted by a view of the surrounding area, including a view of far-off Bengbu. I could see another rocky summit beyond where the quarry was located. My friend told me that once the two hills were connected and were one mountain, but when the quarry was dynamited, the hills had become two partitions. He told me that we could not go to the other hill, because it was a military area, but that once it had been the site of the ancient temple. Behind the hill, looking out in one direction, was a meteorological radar station with a unique ball-shaped architecture. Below the mountain, there was a large chemical plant.

We then descended the hill to a cave opening near the quarry. I was told that the cave was used during *World War Two* to store military equipment so that it could not be seen by the Japanese, but that now it was used to grow mushrooms. We entered the cave where we were hailed by the mushroom grower, who gave us a flashlight so that we could explore further. With the flashlight, we were able to walk for about ten minutes through the rock-strewn cave until our steps became blocked by a small stream. We then exited, and climbed back up the hill to the temple and to our bicycles.

Over the course of the next few months, I would ride my bike to the temple to pray. During that time, I met the few monks and nuns who lived there, including one young volunteer who spoke English. She told me that there was a Buddhist master in residence, but that he was usually traveling to obtain funds for the new temple. I would often go to the temple for lunch and was always greeted kindly. I would sit with the people from the temple, and often with the construction workers building the temple, and eat the simple but delicious vegetarian meals. I enjoyed the spiritual atmosphere and peace of the temple.

Another religious group, whom I would see whenever I took the bus into Bengbu were the Huai people who are Muslims. The Huai people are one of the fifty-six recognized ethnic groups in China. I could always recognize them because the men wear white hats and the women…head scarves. I would see many of them working in their restaurants or in vending stalls in the streets. There were also two old mosques in the city center with the distinctive crescent and star atop the mosque. The Huai people, like many other people, came to China along the Silk Road to trade, but mixed with the Mongol and Han people and stayed. The Huai are different from many minorities in China because they speak Chinese, and not their own language.

These encounters with other religions were very interesting to me, and my time in China was made more interesting by encounters with people from other faiths.

Rock Star

I entered the classroom to shouts and cheering from a hundred students. The chalkboard was covered with multicolored balloons and blinking Christmas lights. I was attending an English Corner Association gathering on a Friday night at Bengbu College. As part of my contract, I was to attend student extracurricular events, like "The English Corner," as needed. The student leaders and organizers of the English Corner shook my hand and guided me to my seat as I waved hello to the assembled students. I was brought a soda drink, candy, and sunflower seeds. The students leaders, who spoke fluent English, announced the schedule for the evening, which included games, new vocabulary, and a free English conversation period with the honored guest—yours truly. Then I was asked to come forward and to give a little talk about who I was and where I was from.

As I walked to the front of the class, I was met with more cheers as students began to take my picture with their cell phones. I told the students how honored I was to be a teacher at the college, and how welcomed I felt by everyone. I also said that I was from Oregon in the United States, and did my pantomime using my hands—showing them where California was with my bottom hand, and Oregon atop of that much known state. My presentation was followed by more cheers and clapping. Being the modest American that I am, I refrained from doing my Mick Jagger imitation of strutting across the stage, or my Peter Townsend routine of leaping into the air only to descend and to break my guitar against the ground! Nonetheless, I was definitely a rock star to the students.

According to *Wikipedia*, the English Corner Association began twenty-five years ago in Shenyang City, of Liaoning Province, when a student who was reading an English book—while waiting on a street corner for a traffic light to change—began a conversation with another student. They agreed to meet at the same corner the next week to speak and to learn English together. Thus, the creation of an "English Corner." The English Corner Association denotes "informal periods of instruction in English held at schools or colleges in China. These sessions are led by native Chinese teachers. The emphasis is on improving the oral language skills of the participants." (*Wikipedia*).

After my stellar introduction, the student leaders had the students play charades. Volunteers from the crowd came forward, and one student was given an English phrase which they had to pantomime so that the other students could guess the English words. This was very hilarious to all of the students and the atmosphere was very joyous. Of course, it didn't take long before I was asked to come forward to participate. My performance in trying to guess the English words was less than perfect, but as a celebrity, I could do no wrong. More photography ensued!

Next, several English words were written on the blackboard, and the students were invited to guess the meaning of the arcane English words. This proved to be a challenge to the students, who were from all the departments of the college. Most of them were not English majors, but the student leaders coaxed them into a relative understanding of their meaning. Clearly, the goal was to increase the students' English vocabulary.

As I sat watching these events, students sitting around me engaged me in conversation. They were obviously enthralled to be speaking to a foreigner and were hesitant, at first, to speak to me; but their cohorts would urge them to stammer the usual questions. "Where are you from?" "Do you like China?" "Do you like Chinese food?" "Are you lonely being away from your family?" This quizzical litany followed the normal pattern, until the magical moment that everyone was waiting for arrived.

The student leaders announced that the free talk part of the program had arrived, and that everyone could speak to the night's celebrity. I was led from one group of students to another who would inevitably say, "She's a shy girl, and is afraid to talk." After reassuring the student, I would try to say something meaningful, and ask where they were from and what they were studying in school. I really enjoyed talking to the students who were so sweet and welcoming. I made my procession around the classroom like any famous Hollywood star would, sharing my celebrity and light with the students.

Like any rock star, the students took many pictures with me, arm in arm—smiles all around. Often it was whole groups who would take pictures with me. Then the moment came, when I was asked for my autograph. Yes, me, Michael Siems, the boy who grew up in Melvindale, Michigan, USA, signed his autograph. This was followed by many more autographs and pictures until I had completed my kingly rounds.

Finally, the night was over as the student leaders announced my departure. I waved my farewell to the assembled masses, as they cheered. A new star had been born! Would the world ever be the same? Then, my student handlers walked me home across the campus to my mansion. I was famous!

The Holy Temple of Kobe

During my time at Bengbu College, the importance of physical education and sports in Chinese life was very apparent. Everywhere you went on campus, students and teachers were engaged in some form of physical activity. You would see students playing badminton, usually women students, behind walls at the library to block the ever-present wind. Some students would be playing ping-pong in the student union, where there were four ping-pong tables. These were usually the students who were masters of one of the Chinese peoples' national sport. Other students, who were less able, played ping-pong on the three tables located outside, next to the women's dormitories. But the majority of students, or several hundreds of men, would be playing basketball at the basketball courts, every day and in all types of weather. Yes, basketball is an obsession for most of the students, and they spend most of their spare time at the hoops. Other students would be playing soccer on the athletic field, while others would be engaged in practicing Kung Fu exercises, often with nunchucks. Many students would always be running around the track or doing stretches for physical education classes.

I soon learned, when teaching my classes, how important basketball—and especially the National Basketball Association—was to students. Many of the students said that they stayed up during the night hours to watch NBA games from America. This was true for men and women students. The students are basketball crazy! Of course, the Houston Rockets basketball team is a favorite because of the Chinese star, Yao Ming; but no one is comparable to the almighty god of basketball, Kobe Bryant. All of the students follow his exploits with the Los Angeles Lakers, and admire him for his "bravery and honesty." It is not an understatement to say that the students worship at the Holy Temple of Kobe. This is a universal phenomenon, and I remembered reading once of how, when some members of various teams from the NBA visited China, they were treated like gods. Now, I understood!

When they asked me whether I liked basketball, they were disconsolate when I told them that I liked baseball, not basketball. I think my star status fell a little from the Chinese sky, but it is true that many men in America from my generation prefer baseball. I was a true-blooded American. I remember the one time that I attended an NBA game in Detroit when the Detroit Pistons were playing. I was bored to tears: who could love a game when each team scores almost every time? I know this is shortsighted in many people's eyes, and was especially so in those of my Chinese students. However, for me, there is nothing more exciting than a well pitched baseball game.

Nonetheless, all of the sports action on campus took place every day with most of the male students bouncing and shooting basketballs at the many courts. Not many women students played the game, but would rather watch all of the future Yao Mings making their lay-ups and three-pointers. I asked one student why they liked basketball so much. He said, "Because it is easy to get a few guys together to play a game anywhere." I guess that made sense to me; and their enthusiasm was infectious.

Soon after coming to the college, foolish me tried to play table tennis with the big guys—the local Chinese players. I was soon disabused of this idea, as I watched these experts spin and smash the ping-pong ball every time! It was simply amazing to watch the speed and agility with which they played the game. Of course, many of these same players had been playing the game since they were little children. Nonetheless, one day I played several games in the student union with one of the local hotshots. I was no competition for him; but, occasionally I would rally enough to score a point, surprising him. I had fun, though, and by the time the exercise was over I was wringing wet from the sweat. As I left, I assured my opponent that we would play again, but I never did play in the union again.

I relegated my ping-pong playing to the three tables outside where the less skilled players adjourned. That being said, really these students excelled at the game too, but only to a lesser degree than the students in the union. I was able to play with them, and enjoyed my many ping-pong matches where I honed my American skills with the "Chinese team." Sometimes, children as young as eight or nine would challenge us; and many times they were our superiors. Both men and women would play outside, and all of them had a great level of expertise. After all, it is the Chinese national sport!

Everywhere on campus, people played the other Chinese favorite: badminton. They would slash at the birdie as if it were some real bird to be vanquished. Chinese badminton, like ping pong, is played in China with a passion and excellence not seen elsewhere in the world. At Bengbu College, it was always difficult to play, because of the ceaseless wind, but people would always find a corner behind a wall or building to play.

In class, students asked me if I had watched the 2008 Beijing Olympics; and when I told them that I had not, their faces showed their disbelief and dismay. I told them that I was traveling at the time and was unable to see the games. Other students asked me whether I knew certain Chinese Olympic stars, and their faces showed their astonishment that I did not know any of them. For the students, as with China as a whole, the 2008 Olympics had been the subject of intense national pride, and was a showcase for China's modernization. So, in some ways, I was a pariah for not having watched the games!

The 2008 Olympic Summer Games were held in Beijing from August 8th, and up through the 24th. According to *Wikipedia*, China became the eighteenth nation to hold the summer games, and only the third Asian nation to hold an Olympics. The Chinese were very proud that they took the most gold medals, with fifty-one of them and one hundred medals altogether.

The build-up to the 2008 Olympics in China had been tremendous. Of the thirty-seven venues used, thirty-one had been constructed prior to the games. Between 15 to 40 billion dollars were spent in preparation for the events where twenty-eight sports and three hundred and two events would be held. A million people, particularly young people, were trained as volunteers to greet the foreigners who would come to the games. The opening and closing ceremonies were magical extravaganzas. It was not just a sports event, but rather a political showcase for modern China. So, for a *laowai,* like me, to have said that he had not watched the games was unbelievable to my students' ears.

During my classes, invariably, and again and again, the students would bring up their pride in China for hosting the Olympic games. Each time the games were mentioned, the students would almost become emotional about it. I was learning about the pride of the Chinese people in all of their accomplishments. I had much to learn.

One day, a student told me that classes were going to be cancelled for three days because of an upcoming athletic meet. I did not know what to make of his statement, and found it to be so inconceivable that the administration would cancel classes for a sporting event. When I asked my advisor about it, he confirmed to me that, indeed, classes were to be canceled due to an Olympic-style track event that the college had held every year. When I said that I would like to attend the event, I was as mistaken as saying that I'd wanted to run in the events with other teachers. I assured Derrick, my advisor, that I had only wanted to be in attendance for the pure excitement of watching everyone, because I would probably die if I'd tried to run against other athletes!

The day of the Bengbu College Olympics had arrived, and it was very much a major campus event. For the opening ceremonies, all of the departments marched around the field behind giant flags, which denoted the colors of the teams. Martial music blared from loudspeakers as the announcer heralded the events. What followed were three days of track and field events, with the different school departments competing against each other.

I spent these three days watching my students from the English department compete in the events. It was nice to come to know the students outside of the classroom, and to become friends with some of them. I admired the way that they competed with such enthusiasm. Typical events included all of the various distance races: long jumping, javelin, high jumping, hurdles, long jumping, and shot put. It was very enjoyable to watch the competitions. I marveled when during the 5000-meter race, a Tibetan student ran the race with such aplomb by staying behind the leaders until the last lap, and then by sprinting the last lap to win the race. I had expected this result, because runners who live at high altitudes have a physiological advantage over runners from lower altitudes. Soon, the three days of events were over, and the closing ceremony mirrored the opening ceremony with its colorful flags and marching students.

It was very apparent that sports and physical activity take on a paramount importance on Chinese college campuses. Physical education is part of the curriculum and all students take part in that class. It seemed strange to me, however, that an American sport like basketball was the most popular with students, but I think that was because I was never initiated into the Holy Temple of Kobe!

"There Is No Sandwich"

Each day I would go to the dining hall to take my meals along with the throngs of students. I would stand in front of the one dining counter where I had developed a friendship with the woman server who was regularly there. She was a young woman, in her early thirties, who always had a smile and who always welcomed me. It was like a joke between us that I would watch what the students ordered, and point to the dish that looked appetizing to me. She would then write the order on a little slip of paper in Chinese, and send the order to the cooks in the kitchen behind the counter. When the dish was prepared, she would bring the meal to me, and I would thank her—*"Xiexie!"* That I had made an attempt to speak Mandarin would always elicit laughter from her. This procedure went on for months, and proved to be an effective method for me to order my meals, save for the fact that I was at the mercy of what the students ordered.

One day, I was standing at the counter, waiting to make the gesture that produced my food, when a student who I didn't know looked at me and said, "There is no sandwich." Well, it was difficult for me not to burst out in laughter and to start rolling on the floor in my mirth! That was the funniest thing I had heard since I had come to China. There were many times when I had thought that very same thing—there certainly was no sandwich; and as an American, sometimes I thought about that simple meal that we Americans have enjoyed almost every day as a matter of course. I would dream about sandwiches of all kinds: turkey, chicken, avocado, tuna, cheese, and grilled cheese. Unfortunately, my fantasies had to find requital in my dreams because I was in the land of rice and noodles.

According to *Wikipedia*, "Anhui Cuisine is one of the eight culinary traditions of China. It is derived from the cooking styles of the Huangshan Mountains and is similar to Jiangsu Cuisine." The *Wikipedia* article goes on to say that "Anhui Cuisine is known for its use of wild herbs, both land and sea, and [for its] simple method of preparation. Braising and stewing are common techniques. Frying and stir-frying are used much less commonly." Also, Anhui Cuisine utilizes control of the cooking fire, an emphasis on the use of oil, the color combinations of the dishes, and is famed for the use of wild game and fish. *Wikipedia* also notes that Anhui Cuisine has three styles: Yangtze River, Huai River, and South Anhui. In the Bengbu area where I taught English, Yanhuai Cuisine was particularly spicy hot and salty. I was to find out just how spicy food can be!

During my first weeks at the college, when I was eating in the dining hall, I would order a dish and begin to eat. Suddenly, although it was not visually apparent, I would begin to notice that my mouth was on fire! The rice dish that I was eating was laced with peppers. I am very fond of spicy foods, especially Mexican and Indian foods, and I have been known to eat jalapeño peppers like candy; but these preparations were unlike any that I had encountered before in their volatile spiciness. At least on one occasion, I had to run back to my apartment because my intestines were ready to explode from being upset by the spices. Many of the rice dishes that I would eat had this same deadly quality. For me, however, I grew accustomed to the nuclear intensity of the spices, and generally, eating them did not lead to a chain reaction. I had a good time eating the food in the dining hall.

For breakfast, the dining hall offered a wide assortment of what were called something like *"boza"* by the students, which were steamed buns filled with meat and others with vegetables. Also, there was a moist, flat, dough-like bread that had been steamed and filled with either seaweed or red peppers, which I really liked a lot. Then there were soups and gruels with various grains, and especially a rice-like gruel, which was really good. Seaweed soup was a particular favorite of mine. Of course, there were many egg-type breads and hard-boiled eggs. There was never any fruit, as the students—and the staff, such as myself—had to buy their fruit from vendors.

It is difficult to describe the wide variety of food that was available for lunch and dinner at the dining halls. I think that every variety of food that could have been made available from the Chinese cuisine was there. As previously mentioned, there is a distinction between north and south in China: students from the north ate noodle dishes, and students from the south liked rice dishes. Each floor in a given dining hall had multiple ordering areas where different foods or specialties could be ordered. The students all knew which areas were the cheapest and which had the best quality. In one dining hall, you could order your rice and then pick the kind of vegetable, casserole, tofu, or meat to eat with it. In the dining area that I frequented, there were a variety of choices: dumplings with a meat filling, noodles with a peanut sauce, or a beef noodle soup, and fried noodles with beef…The rice dish area had a myriad of possibilities to go with it, and of course, there were meat dishes like chicken, pork, or duck, and hot pots—a wicker bowl filled with spicy delights. Each floor of the dining hall was different, and if the students had wanted to be extravagant, there was a restaurant with private rooms where they could choose from a menu.

The dining counter where I ate my food had many rice and tofu dishes that I liked, including a spicy tofu dish, *kung pao ji* (kung pao chicken), fried rice, a very spicy eggplant dish, and a spicy cabbage and pepper dish. There were so many wonderful rice dishes.

Naturally, the restaurant was the most expensive choice. A simple rice dish would often just cost between two and six yuan (between thirty cents and less than a dollar). Fish and chicken dishes were more expensive. Eating in the dining hall was very inexpensive. Each student and I held a card like a credit card, upon which you could put as credit as many yuan as you had liked. This card would then be swiped across a machine by a server when you bought your meal. I could eat for more than two weeks on only 100 yuan, or on about fourteen US dollars.

Once I was told by a Chinese friend that the "Chinese people live to eat, rather than [having to] eat to live." She also told me that traditionally women would spend the whole day cooking complicated dishes, so important is food to Chinese culture. Now, with busy modern life, if you go into a large supermarket in China, you will see a vast quantity of cooked items that people will come in to buy for dinner, because they don't have time to cook it themselves. I was told that all of the pre-cooked food is purchased in the market by the end of the day. Eating is such a critical part of Chinese culture. Whenever I went out to eat in the local restaurants, they were always crowded with customers. When I asked a Chinese teacher about this, considering that the economy even in China was bad, he said, "The people would rather spend their money on eating in restaurants than on anything else." Another example of this was in the classroom. When I asked the students to introduce themselves upon having first met them, several students used this phrase to describe themselves, "I am like a little pig—I like to eat and sleep." And they did not mean this in a pejorative sense: they thought this was a very practical and good approach to life! Although I was at first taken aback by this, I learned how central eating was to Chinese people. As I have said, usually one of the first things I would be asked when I met people was whether I liked Chinese food, quickly followed by whether I liked rice or noodles.

I went through many mental culinary journals during my time in China. There were periods when I thought to myself about how I could never eat another dish of rice. This was against the background of having eaten rice so frequently in America. Rice and stir-fried vegetables is one of my favorite dishes, but I longed for the variety of the cuisines to be found in America. In America, I could go out to a Thai, a Mexican, an Indian, an Italian, or to a seafood restaurant—and I missed this extravagance of the American palette. I longed for spaghetti and I longed for burritos! Mostly, however, I really enjoyed the Chinese cuisine and made a temporary peace with my American appetites.

Sometimes, I would satisfy my various cravings by buying tuna, mayonnaise, potato chips and bread at the grocery store in the city center, and have an American lunch. Or at other times, I would make spaghetti at home in my kitchen, but this was infrequent.

The students would ask me if I liked the food in the dining halls. I always said that I really liked the food. Then they would say that they did not like it at all, especially if they had been there for more than one year. They would then tell me that they ate at the vendors, located in the vendor tent-covered area near the campus. Indeed, there were always students streaming there at meal times. If they wanted to be particularly extravagant, they would dine at the many restaurants located in the Longzihu shopping area near the other universities.

Over the course of several months, my relationship with my friend—the woman server at the dining hall—developed. She came to know which dishes I liked, and would joke with me about wanting tofu or eggplant. Then, an English student of mine helped her to write the Chinese and English names in her yellow notebook. Subsequently, whenever I came to her counter, she would pull out her book and I could point to one of the four dishes written there. My communication abilities were improving, and I was becoming less of a *laowai* baby! I was actually able to choose some foods that I liked. I kept telling myself... *"Wait until you go home to America."* I dreamed of fresh salads and avocados. They were coming!

The Borg

The curriculum that I devised for my first semester at Bengbu College was largely interactive and designed for the students to come to know me, and for me to know them. I would use different mediums: the visual, the auditory, the poetic, the current-affairs style, the inspirational, and still others to understand my students better. In addition, I would have them write a short paragraph each week describing their interests. I had ascertained almost immediately that the students, with possibly a few exceptions in between, had all had a collective mind in their vision of life.

Their visual representations of who they were mirrored this consistent theme of collectivity. Many students in different classes showed the same cartoon popular in China about a little sheep and his friends. I was amazed that college students were interested in cartoons, but all of them were enthralled when these cartoon characters were projected on the screen. Other students showed pictures of the 2009 Szechuan earthquake, actual pictures of dead bodies in the rubble. These students would get highly emotional and even the male students would begin crying when they saw the pictures. This seemed extraordinary to me that there was that degree of affinity with the whole nation. Then there were many students who showed pictures of their families, especially pictures of little children, whom they would tell elaborate stories about. This re-emphasized to me just how important the family is in China.

The music class in which students played music from their favorite popular musical groups was very revealing of the students' mutual interests. They all liked the same pop stars and by and large, like young women everywhere, they revered Asian male pop stars who were young and handsome. Some especially liked Korean pop stars. One student explained that she was targeted by other students for liking a non-Chinese pop star, and began sobbing in class because of this treatment. Then, over and over the students played the music from the movie, *Titanic*: "My Heart Will Go On" by Celine Dion. Most unusually, the students played this one American pop song from the 1960's, "We Had Seasons in the Sun," that their elementary teachers' liked and had played for them. While it is not unusual for students anywhere in the world to like the same music, it was strange that there was almost a cult-like knowledge and admiration for certain songs. Some students even stood up in front of the class and sang these same songs. Most interesting to me was that none of the students had heard of Bob Dylan! Yes, there is a place in the world where Mr. Zimmerman is unknown.

In one class, I had them bring in their favorite poets. Again, in all of the classes, the same poets were extolled. Shakespeare, Wordsworth, and Keats were the favorites; but there was a smattering of other poets, such as Robert Frost and Rabindranath Tagore, which had surprised me. Tagore in particular was a surprise, as he was a favorite of mine, but they all knew this same poem by him. Then there were a few Chinese poets that they had read and enjoyed, but generally these were not the classical Chinese poets known all over the world, but usually a poet that they had been exposed to in high school. They would all recite the same poems!

A vision of the collective-student Chinese mind began to dawn on my consciousness when we discussed literature. Every single student loved Romantic classical novels, like those of the Brontë Sisters. It was almost like Emily and Charlotte Brontë were the hottest modern novelists. Jane Eyre and Wuthering Heights were on the *Top Ten Best Sellers* for Chinese English students. The women students all said that either Jane Eyre or Gone With the Wind were their favorite novels. I wondered at how this could be, but I then realized that the only literature really available to students in China was the classic literature.

That being said, there were of few "modern novels" that everyone seemed to have read, such as Hemmingway's The Old Man and the Sea, but this was an exception. It was more apparent that Charles Dickens' world of A Tale of Two Cities was more current than the modern world.

I really became intrigued when we did the class on inspirations. I came to understand that, in the Chinese educational system, only certain books were read: they must all have the same textbooks, and all of the teachers must talk about the same things! What they had created was a collective Chinese student mind. For instance, many of the students said that they'd loved Audrey Hepburn. They did not know her from her movies, but rather for her charitable work. This really flabbergasted me! Audrey *Hep*-burn? They had all heard Martin Luther King's *"I Have a Dream"* speech, and many of them knew about Mahatma Gandhi. Another favorite heroine was Helen Keller, who was known for her ability to overcome her multiple handicaps. China's current political leaders, Hu Jintao and Wen Jiabao, and from the past, Zhao En Lai, were almost iconic emotional paragons to the students. In one class, we talked about what famous person they would love to have dinner with—and it was unanimous with students that these Chinese leaders would be ideal. Surprisingly, Mao Tse Tung was rarely mentioned.

In another class, we discussed where each student would like to travel. The United States was mentioned most frequently. New York City, Las Vegas, and places in California topped their lists. Some students showed pictures of homes and places in which they would like to live in the future. These two-story homes, located in wooded areas, were always in America. The students had an idealized view of America that had been based on movies, television, and the NBA. Their vision was that everyone is rich and happy. I tried to disabuse them of this notion by telling them about the poverty, the gun violence, and social ills of America such as: drugs, mental illness, and disease. I asked some students why America was so desirable, and they said, "Because America has what we want." It was very clear that the Chinese student-vision of heaven was an American one.

Then the statements that students made in class were as if they were parroting party slogans that they were taught by their teachers and parents. They all talked about "never giving up." This was stated over and over, class after class, just like a slogan. Also, they talked about how—even if they had failed or were sad—that they would persist and keep going, while having a positive attitude in and through all of the ups and the downs. I must admit that I really liked these positive mindsets in my students because they obviously believed them and lived their lives accordingly. This, to me, was in contrast to the cynical and sarcastic, negative minds of many modern youth. Then, the most revealing statement that I could place within this strain of my thought was that whenever the country of China was mentioned, they all said, *"Our China,"* not China, but "Our China." It became very clear that the two most important things in their lives were the country of China and their families. Everything in their lives revolved and was formed around these two things; everything else was secondary.

This collective student mind was in every way secular. No one talked about religion in any context. Two students did openly say that they were Christian, but they were the exception. During one class on supernatural phenomena, several of the students told stories about their grandparents as having healed them by taking them to the Buddhist temple, or as having healed them with herbs. Other students told stories about ghosts, and about mysterious lights that they or others saw around tombs. So, there was still a folk knowledge about unexplained phenomena that was alive in rural areas. However, most students said that they did not believe in life after death, and they would always take a secular approach to most subjects when questioned.

This vision of a collective Chinese mind was more than affirmed by the physical closeness and affection that the students showed each other. Also, this correlated with the fact that the Chinese educational system purposely kept the same students in the same classes together over the course of many years so as to create a collective attitude. When you watched the students together it was like seeing a single organism, not individuals.

Another example of this physical closeness was what I experienced on a beach on Putuoshan Island in the East China Sea. It was a beautiful, very long, and sandy beach. All the Chinese people, hundreds of them, were in one very small swimming area of the beach. From there on, though—sprawling all of the way out—was a long stretch of beach with no one on it! Of course, as Americans, my friend and I chose to be at the far end of the beach where there were no people. It was obvious that the Chinese people wanted to be together on the beach as a group, and derived comfort in the crowd.

Then, I remembered the American science-fiction television program, *"Star Trek, The Next Generation,"* which, in some of the programs, showcased an alien race bent on subjugating the universe: "The Borg." According to *Wikipedia*, in the TV series, "The Borg manifest as cybernetically enhanced humanoid drones of multiple species, organized as an interconnected collective, the decisions of which are made by a hive mind." The article goes on to say that in American pop culture, the Borg are synonymous with a force against which "resistance is futile." In my mind, the Chinese students seemed to function in a hive-mind context. As I had already related in an earlier section of this book, whenever questioned all of the individuals around the person would translate and offer suggestions and answers to the given question. In any other country, especially in the West, the student who had been put in the spotlight would be left to stand and answer the question alone, or to be left to fall back into the shade of not knowing, but not in China. In China, the collective mind, the Borg mind, is operative. In my eyes, and I believe in reality, this student mind is simply a reflection and a part of the greater Chinese collective societal mind, which has greater implications for the world.

Chang'e

After an hour-long ferry ride from Ningbo, a city in Zhejiang Province, I was approaching Putuoshan Island—an island south east of Shanghai in the East China Sea. I could see the 33-meter high golden statue of Quan Yin, the Buddhist goddess of compassion, on top of a hill overlooking the island. As the ferry docked at the wharf, there was a sign in Chinese, which a friend had translated as reading, "Of all the places in the world, this is the purest." And it certainly was that—one of the most beautiful places I have visited in all of my travels, and a Chinese national park.

There had been an almost week-long break from classes at Bengbu College that had been set aside to celebrate China's National Day, October 1st—and the Chinese Autumn Festival. It was the sixtieth anniversary of the establishment of Communist China, and the government was celebrating it with military parades and gala extravaganzas in Beijing, which were televised nationally. I decided to spend the holidays on Putuoshan Island, which I had visited on two previous trips to China. I learned quickly, in trying to plan the trip, that traveling during the Autumn Festival would not be easy.

The Chinese Autumn Festival is one of the main holidays, along with the Spring Festival, when all Chinese people travel to their homes to be with their families for feasts, and to celebrate the harvest. Consequently, most people are either traveling by rail or by bus to their home cities. What makes this possible is that journeying by rail or by bus is relatively inexpensive. China has an extensive modern rail system, which allows the common citizen to journey anywhere in China. For instance, I could travel from Bengbu to Shanghai, Beijing, or even to Tibet easily. In China, you cannot purchase a rail ticket to a given destination until ten days prior to your travel. As a result, when I tried to buy a ticket, I could only get a ticket from Bengbu to Shanghai, but not to Ningbo, where I was to catch the ferry going onwards. And so, I made the decision that I would take a taxi to Ningbo, which was going to cost about $125. It was going to be an expensive vacation to Putuoshan Island!

When I got to the Bengbu train station for my journey to Shanghai, I could not believe how many people were in the station. There were people everywhere, carrying huge bags with bedding, produce, grains, and with everything except for live chickens and pigs! It was amazing to see that all of China was on the move, which was apparent by the fact that many groups of people were mothers, fathers, children, and grandparents—the whole extended family. When the lights began to flash with the number for the train to Shanghai, people began jumping over the chairs to get to the head of the "line" that was there in front of the gate to enter for boarding. It was chaos! I followed the stream of people to the correct platform, at which juncture the conductor had helped me find the correct train. When I neared my seat, I noted that a young man was sitting in my seat. When I motioned politely to him that the seat was my seat, he acted as though I could have asked him to walk to Shanghai instead. He moved, and sat with a large group of people and some extended family, traveling all together.

During the journey to Shanghai, it was fascinating to watch the people entering and exiting the train. During the Autumn Festival, it was very important for Chinese families to be together—not unlike the time of our Christmas or Thanksgiving, where it is a nice thing if families are together. My students had told me how important to the Chinese people the festival has been: families would be able to maintain their familiar bonds. The family is the central feature of Chinese society, unlike the corresponding structure in America in which the individual often takes precedence.

I marveled at the beauty of the Chinese countryside as the train slowly made its way to Shanghai. My problem on the train was that I had a suitcase and a backpack with me, and being by myself, I felt unsafe in leaving them to go to the restroom. So, for most of the journey, I sat with my backpack in my lap, and my suitcase in the overhead rack. The family that sat in seats near me fully utilized the train and ate the snacks that they had brought for their journey. When they exited the train outside of Shanghai, the piles of sunflower-seed husks, eggshells, and package wrappers trailed around us all as if to mark the progress of the People's Liberation Army on the Long March. After having been ten hours on the train, I was so happy to see the city of Shanghai approaching, as the train made its way through the miles and miles of high-rise apartments.

Shanghai at night is a jewel to behold, with each building adorned with many colored lights: it was like a city of Christmas trees. When I exited the train station, I was happy to find the driver with my name on a sign, ready to take me on my drive to Ningbo.

In 2007, the distance from Shanghai to Ningbo had been shortened from 249 miles to 75 miles by the completion of the Hangzhou Bay Bridge—a twenty-two mile long structure across Hangzhou Bay. As we approached the bridge, I saw fireworks celebrating the national holiday. After a roundabout drive through much construction, my driver finally found my hotel in Ningbo. I was happy to see that it was a nice hotel, and that I would have a good night's rest before the ferry ride to Putuoshan Island in the morning.

My stay on Putuoshan Island was pleasant, as I enjoyed the semi-tropical surroundings, the monasteries, and the many restaurants on the island. It is a jewel of a national park, which is marked by two beautiful beaches, mountains, and also by a few forests. The island is very clean, and not littered with garbage and trash, like many other places in China. The island has a convenient bus system that transports tourists all over the island. Many Buddhists from around the world come to the island to worship Quan Yin in her many temples. There is a tangible feeling of peace and compassion, especially when walking on the moonlit roads along the ocean at night. During my stay, there was a festive atmosphere as the throngs of tourists enjoyed the Autumn Festival, and the beauty of the moon goddess, Chang'e, as she shone over the East China Sea.

My four-star hotel was situated near the beach, and had a view of the ocean from its well-stationed balcony. It was a perfect spot to spend the Autumn Festival and to do some moon watching—Chang'e in all of her glory. The rare and autumnal earth had been kissed in the moon's light, and everything that one could pass their eyes upon was moon-kissed. My dear students had related to me the myth of Chang'e, which is an ancient Chinese fable. Chang'e might be said today to be the Chinese equivalent of a "man in the moon," albeit the female version of that... "the woman in the moon."

The story is told that Chang'e and her husband, Hougi, the archer, were immortals. In that long-forgotten time of historical antiquity, the Jade emperor had ten sons, who one day, by dint of a terrible and terrific magic, had transformed into real suns. Unfortunately, their heat was burning up the Earth, and so the Jade Emperor asked Hougi to shoot them out of the sky. Hougi, instead of shooting down all ten of the suns, left one sun in the sky.

The Jade Emperor, in his anger, banished Hougi and Chang'e to the earth, and took away their immortality. Chang'e was upset by this loss. So, Hougi traveled to the Queen Mother of the West, who gave him a pill that would restore their immortality, one half for Hougi and one half for Chang'e. One day, however, Hougi was away and Chang'e became curious about the pill. By the time that Chang'e had taken the pill out of its case, Hougi had returned unexpectedly. Chang'e—fearful of being discovered—swallowed the whole pill. She immediately began floating up to the moon, where she remains until today in her immortality.

During the Autumn Festival, Chinese families gather together and have big feasts. At night, they sit outside, tell stories, eat moon cakes and moon pies, and gaze at Chang'e in her full glory. It is a celebration of the autumn harvest and of the full fall moon.

Every evening, I sat on my balcony and followed the tradition of the Autumn Festival, and ate moon cakes and pies of many flavors: osmanthus, rose, lavender, and sesame. What a treat it was to watch Chang'e move her gracious form over the ocean, to eat delicious treats, and to listen to the waves. It was magic under the stars! The wisdom of China is not only ancient, but it is mystical in its closeness to nature and to the seasons. There was certainly a feeling of oneness with the world, and a connection between human beings and nature.

One morning, I watched the sun rise over the sea, together with many other tourists and islanders who had gathered on the beach for this daily miracle. The sun suddenly popped out of the gray ocean fog—a red globe coming to warm the new day. From having lived on the West coast of America, I had always imagined what it would be like to see the sunrise on the other side of the ocean—and, on that misty ocean morning, I had lived to realize my dream.

One afternoon, I went to the beach near the hotel to go swimming. The waves were huge, perhaps seven to eight feet tall at times—perfect for body surfing! It was such a wonderful feeling of freedom to surge with the waves to the shore, out and in for hours. Soon, people had gathered on the beach to watch me, and to take videos of my performance. What fun!

Another morning, I got up before sunrise, and went to the Fayu Monastery which was near my hotel. I sat in the darkness outside of one of the gates, hoping to hear the monks chant their morning worship. As the waves crashed below, and the wind blew the leaves in the trees, the celestial chanting of the monks was heralded by the beating of huge drums. Then, the monks began singing the sweetest lullaby to the goddess of compassion, Quan Yin. It was a beautiful dream filled with heavenly sounds that helped the sun to rise, and as I opened my eyes, I could see men sweeping the temple steps to begin the new day.

Every day I went to the monasteries on the island: the Fayu Monastery with its dragon wall, the Puji Monastery with its ancient camphor trees, and to the Huiji Monastery atop the mountain. One evening, I joined a group of Buddhist nuns and worshippers, who were doing full prostrations while circumambulating the Puji Monastery. After several rounds, I returned to my hotel room, only to discover in the mirror that I had had a quarter-sized hole in the center of my forehead from touching my head to the hallowed ground! I have always enjoyed climbing the thousands of steps up the mountain to the Huiji Monastery, from where you could have spectacular views of the island and the ocean. Putuoshan is not only a place of pilgrimage, but also one of the beautiful gems of China.

It was with sadness that after three days, I returned by ferry to Ningbo, where I was to catch the train for my overnight journey back to Bengbu. It had been a magical Autumn Festival, and a well-deserved vacation from school; but it was time to return to the college and to my teaching duties.

Fireworks in the Night

One of the joys of my stay in China was the almost nightly display of fireworks. The Chinese love fireworks of all kinds, the evidence for which is that they are used year-round to celebrate and to commemorate births, deaths, marriages, and business openings. The Chinese New Year is an unsurpassingly majestic...the ultimate time for fireworks, and everyone joins in the fun with the whole world turning into one big explosion. On any night, I would be sitting in my office when I would hear the explosions begin in the villages. I would look out of the window and watch the skyrockets in the night: reds, golds, white blares, whirls, followed by their cracks and booms. I asked a Chinese friend how much these skyrockets had cost, and he told me that they were not inexpensive—some costing as much as ten dollars a skyrocket! I was surprised because the villages were very poor, and I wondered where they had gotten the money for such extravagance. My friend assured me that the Chinese loved fireworks so much that price was no barrier to the celebration of any event in which fireworks would need to be featured.

Many mornings would begin with the sound of firecrackers exploding outside of my apartment. Not just a few firecrackers, but long strings of firecrackers were exploded for weddings, births, and deaths. When I was in Bengbu city, everywhere I would see firecrackers exploding, especially in front of hotels and businesses. When you were walking and the firecrackers started to explode, you had to shield your eyes to protect them from errant missiles.

The Chinese were the first people to develop fireworks as a natural extension of the invention of gunpowder. According to *Wikipedia*, "The earliest documentation of fireworks dates back to 7th century China where they were first used to frighten away evil spirits with their loud sound and also to pray for happiness and prosperity." Up until the 14th century, they were usually enjoyed and displayed at the sole discretion of royalty, but by the Ming Dynasty, they had become a common feature of Chinese life and were used for all celebrations.

I really admired the Chinese zest for life, and such a vivid way of announcing an important event. On many Chinese streets, I would always see the aftermath of these activities....the streets strewn with the bright red wrappers from the firecrackers. There were literally firecrackers exploding everywhere.

There have been major problems with fireworks too, such as when every so often a mishap occurs—and a fireworks factory blows up, killing many people. I don't know what the statistics are, but I'm sure that there are many accidents in which people lose fingers, eyes, or even die.

Fireworks, however, are such a prominent feature of Chinese life that is impossible to imagine life there without the ever-present display of color in the night or the robust sound of firecrackers in the day. It is simply one of the highlights of life in China!

Cranes, Not Cranes

As I sped home on the overnight train from Ningbo to Bengbu after my Autumn Festival Holiday, I could see the ongoing construction on the Beijing to Shanghai High Speed Railway that was visible and audible in varying states of rest and activity all along the way, an 819 mile railway due for completion in 2011. The train is slated to travel between 210-240 miles an hour as it charges between China's two major economic zones. I could see where construction had gone directly through villages, which were bulldozed into rubble to make way for the new railway. It was obvious that construction is going on twenty-four hours a day. Near where I live at Bengbu College, a new train station for the rail line is being constructed. Many nights, as I lay in my bed trying to sleep, I would hear explosions at the nearby rail site as dynamite exploded. The whole apartment building and windows would shake. People at the college told me how excited they are about the completion of the railway, but that it is going to be very expensive to take the train: $100 from Bengbu to Shanghai. For me, the building of the railway characterized the rapid modernization of China. There are not many countries that would allow explosions in the night!

I remember traveling from Tunxi to Huangzhou on one of my journeys, and I was impressed by the near fifty-mile construction zone in one area. Watching the growth in China is like watching an army of ants going busily about their constant routines. China is one big construction zone!

Take for instance the apartments where I lived at Bengbu College. Many of them were empty or under construction. I was always hearing buzzing and banging even into the evening as the workers proceeded to finish the apartments. It was never-ending. On many areas of the campus, bulldozers worked to move the earth in preparation for more college buildings. Everywhere around the three college campuses, high-rise apartment buildings rose up like mushrooms on a warm spring night.

Construction of high-rise apartment buildings, where most people live in China, is a priority for the country because of an apartment shortage. Many people told me about the high cost of buying an apartment—the price per square foot for an apartment is astronomical. I was told that most people cannot afford to even buy an apartment, and, consequently, end up renting. One teacher told me that the progressive goal in most men's lives was "first a job, then a wife, then an apartment, and hopefully a car." It was common knowledge that it is easier to be a woman because the social pressure that the man feels to buy an apartment for the family does not hang over her fate in the same way. Of course, I had read elsewhere that there is another social problem, in that twenty-four million Chinese men face life as a bachelor, because of the practice in the countryside of aborting female fetuses in favor of having males, who will carry on the family name and tradition.

One morning I had risen early to get some work done, which was fortunate because at 7 a.m., the power and phone went off. I went for a ride on my bicycle, when I encountered some students who told me that the power would be off until 9 p.m. that night "due to road construction." Later, I learned that not only had the power been turned off at our college, but at all of the three campuses in the area—for thirty thousand students and faculty! Nowhere else in the world would such a priority to construction be given other than in China. Modernization takes precedence over the lives of students. Despite the inconvenience of being out of communication with the world for a day, I enjoyed the party that ensued that evening—with all the students and faculty outside, enjoying the beauty of the night by lighting candles.

China's economy is the fastest growing economy in the world with a gross national product of $4.91 trillion. It is also the third largest economy in the world, behind only the United States and Japan. There is a dynamic sense of optimism and growth, which pervades the atmosphere of the country. It reminds me of the United States during the time that I was growing up in the 1950's and 1960's; it has the same passionate vision that a wonderful future is ahead for the nation. In many ways, it is an exciting place to live and to work because of that vision. There is hope, not despair!

You experience that visually when you visit major Chinese cities, because all of the cities have a futuristic skyline. The architecture is so unlike the architecture in the West. You feel just like you are walking into the future itself with all of the spires, balls, and adornments on all of the buildings. Then, there are the cranes. Yes, 'cranes' as in building cranes, not the birds. Everywhere that you may set your eyes upon the sky, there are cranes atop buildings that are being constructed with such rapidity that you feel that they must have risen overnight. I remember listening to a newscast on National Public Radio, and leaning more attentively into the details of the program when the commentator had said that during the hours after sunset of those years that he had lived in Beijing in the 1980's, there were no lights—only darkness. China has made that much progress! China truly is one large construction zone.

The Rice Fields Are Burning

When I returned to Bengbu after my week on the coast of China, the harvest was in full progress in the Anhui countryside. In fact, the streets were literally flowing with rice as the farmers spread the harvested rice in the streets and bike lanes to dry. This method of drying the rice surprised me, and also made it difficult for me to ride my bicycle without running over the rice. Everywhere you went, however, the streets were covered with the bountiful harvest. In the rice fields themselves, you could see all of the farmers busy with the harvest.

I returned to the classroom to resume the fall classes. Then one morning it began. I looked out of my office window and noticed that the rice fields behind my building were burning. Not only behind my building, but everywhere I looked, I saw smoke rising from the fields as the farmers burned the vegetation remaining from the harvest. It was a true conflagration, smoke and flames everywhere. Soon, you could not see the sky, because of all of the smoke that had limited visibility to a few hundred feet. The smoke became so thick that it looked like fog on a London street. It was difficult to breathe no matter what you were doing: everyone was choking and coughing from the pollution. This went on day after day for several weeks with no abatement.

At the same time I had a sore throat, which may or may not have been due to the smoke in the air, but I was experiencing serious vertigo, because of whatever mysterious thing I had experienced during this time. I would be teaching, attempting to listen to the student's answer my questions, but I was so dizzy that I would have to hold onto a desk to stand up. I was afraid that I was going to hear a student exclaim, "*Tim*-ber!" as their teacher fell face-forward to hit the floor. Indeed, one day I was playing ping-pong with a friend, and became so dizzy that I started to collapse. They raced over, and held me so that I would not fall. That ended playing sports for that day. I did not know what to do to alleviate my dizziness. This state continued for over two weeks, during which time the smoky holocaust continued in the fields around me. There were many days on which I had felt like I was going to have to leave the classroom because of my vertigo. All of the students experienced health problems from the smoke and complained in class about the pollution.

One night, I looked out of my window to see that the mountains were burning. The farmers had ignited the mountaintops, and they burned with orange flames against the darkness. It was beautiful in an apocalyptic way. Everyone enjoys a good bonfire, but it was like the whole world was on fire. During my time in China, I was to learn how much people just liked to burn things. It seemed that a day did not pass without someone lighting a fire in the fields behind my apartment building. Of course, it is an ancient practice to burn the vegetation in the fields to clear them for planting, but when everyone is doing it, it creates a fiery nightmare.

From the time that I arrived in China in August of 2009, I wondered how I was going to live for ten months while breathing the fumes and pollution that is the everyday atmosphere breathed by Chinese lungs. For me, it was like "déjà vu all over again" and I could hear my lungs saying, *"This is like Detroit in the 1960's."* Yes, it was exactly like the industrial area, where I grew up in downriver Detroit, near the Ford Rouge Plant that had produced all of those automobiles many years ago. The air itself smelled like burning chemicals. I would wake up in the morning in my apartment, and try to isolate where the chemical smells were coming from on that day. Sometimes, it was definitely from the many factories that were just miles from the campus, but, at other times, it seemed like the toxic atmosphere came from the new flooring in the apartment. Whatever the case had been, I did not know how my beleaguered lungs were going to acclimate to this poisonous environment. Longevity—which the Chinese so highly value—was certainly going to be a casualty in this toxic nightmare.

One only had to look out of the window of my apartment to see the magnitude of pollution in China. Despite the view of the emerald green fields, which one always enjoyed, the ditch filled with water behind the apartment was also used to receive all of the garbage from the college. It was filled with plastic, paper, bricks, and building materials from recent construction. The banks of a nearby small creek were also utilized, in a similar fashion, as the local dump for the villagers. As far as I could tell, there is no landfill in the area. Any convenient ditch or water source was the landfill! So, any water in the area was polluted by what was being thrown into it. I'm sure the chemical fertilizers and pesticides I saw being sprayed on the crops contributed to the toxicity.

The skyline outside my window also emphasized the lack of consciousness when it came to air quality. I could see at least two large smokestacks from brick-producing plants 'hyperventilating' coal smoke. It was apparent that locally there were no air pollution standards: foundries belched clouds of black coal smoke, chemical factories competed with toxic clouds, and other factories of unknown industrial purposes contributed other pollutants. My American lungs gasped under the assault from the many pollutants that the Chinese believed was air to breathe.

One day, when I was walking near Longzihu Lake, the large lake near the University District in Bengbu, I noticed an oil slick in the water, plastic bags, paper, and other garbage floating in the water. I had been told the legend of how Longzihu Lake, which means "Dragon Lake," had been named. According to the legend, a Ming Dynasty emperor was rowing in a boat on the lake one day, when one of his oars dropped into the water.

Suddenly, the oar turned into a dragon, which soared into the sky. Hence, the name, "Dragon Lake." In my heart, I prayed that the dragon in Dragon Lake had still lived despite the pollution. It was hot and I dreamed of just jumping in and going swimming, but I knew that my body would probably just dissolve from all of the chemicals in the water. I knew that all bodies of water in China are not only polluted, but probably toxic. For instance, Lake Chaohu, a large fresh water lake near Hefei, is polluted by phosphorus, and by other chemicals. I felt so sad that people could never go swimming in the summertime, when the heat in Anhui was torrid. I told my students how, in Oregon, the greatest joy is swimming in the pristine rivers, lakes, and streams. Many of my students told me that they did not know how to swim, and I knew why!

Another significant issue, particularly to my virgin American ears, is the noise pollution in the Chinese cities. Every morning at sunrise, I would hear the tractors zooming down the roads from the villages. These tractors are basically a combustion-engine, mounted on a frame without any muffler, of course. Consequently, they can be heard for miles around as they chug down the roads. More problematic are the buses and cars blaring their horns at anything that may appear in front of them—a true cacophony that, for a pedestrian, is deafening.

According to *Wikipedia*, China is home to sixteen of the twenty most polluted cities in the world. A Harvard study indicates that, "Over the next quarter century, there will be 83 million deaths from lung cancer due to cigarette smoke and the burning of indoor fuels." Many Chinese men smoke cigarettes, which are considered almost a social necessity. Also, seven of ten Chinese homes burn coal for fuel. An article from the *USA Today*, on November, 2009, indicated that carbon dioxide pollution jumped 2% in the world, with most of the increase coming from China. This pollution largely comes from burning coal, natural gas, and concrete production.

Another article in *Wikipedia* stated that desertification is also a significant problem in China with 67 kilometers of desert being added each year. In China, dust storms are an increasing problem each year. I witnessed some of the aftereffects of a sandstorm that hit Beijing in the spring of 2010. Dust from these sand storms affect other Asian nations, and even sweep across the Pacific Ocean all the way to the West coast of America.

China is making significant efforts to reduce pollution. In 2008, the Chinese government spent $498 billion for sewage and rubbish treatment. China is a leader in increasing forest cover. The nation has also invested $34.6 billion in clean technology like wind turbines and solar panels. China has also banned the use of free plastic bags in all grocery stores. So, it is encouraging that, despite ongoing modernization, efforts are being made to reverse the toxic environment in China.

"No Man Is an Island"

Robert was a student in one of my oral English classes. He had above average expressive and receptive language skills, and this was significant because most students did not have his abilities. We immediately struck up a friendship, which I learned later he had done with other foreigners who had lived in Bengbu. He asked me if I wanted to visit the local Buddhist temple one weekend. So, he was the student who guided me to the temple and to the cave which is nearby. However, this was just the beginning, in that every weekend we would either ride bikes somewhere or go on an adventure. I jokingly called it the "Bengbu Adventure Club."

We would ride bicycles to downtown Bengbu to see the Huai River, where barges traveled downriver with their goods. I learned quickly that riding bikes in the city was more than a little dangerous, as buses or electric motorcycles whizzed by just a few inches from my legs. I decided not to go downtown by bike again.

Another weekend, we rode our bikes to South Mountain (Lushan Mountain) which was the mountain that I could see from the window of my office. We rode through South Village, and then locked our bikes near some trees so that we could climb the mountain. Although the mountain is not that big, it was a steep climb as we made the ascent. I felt at home, because in Oregon I climbed the local mountains on a regular basis. From the top of the mountain, we saw all of the local villages, and Bengbu itself, on the horizon. What amazed me was to see that there were more small mountains to the south with villages as far as I could see.

On our adventures, Robert always told me about his life as a student, which was nearing an end as he would graduate in January, but then he would study for the exam which would determine if he would be able to continue for his post-graduate studies. In China, examinations are utilized to decide which students are going to proceed in their education. It is the source of much stress for everyone in the Chinese educational system, and Robert was no exception.

Robert was also my source of information about Chinese culture, student life, and just of my understanding of the many things that happened around me. He was invaluable to me during my cultural adjustment in China. He told me so many things about student life, which helped me to understand the students. He was the one who told me how terrified the students were to talk to me when I had first started teaching at the college.

Robert was not a typical Chinese student in that he questioned what he saw as a very limited perspective and secular viewpoint about life that was held by most Chinese students. He was a Christian, and, as a result, his value system was spiritual, not secular like most students. Robert believed that there was so much more to life than just getting married and making money. To him, spiritual goals and life abroad were his foundation, not the ordinary life of a Chinese citizen. Most of all, he wanted to travel—to see the beauty of China and the world. Like most students, he had never seen the ocean or the major Chinese cities, like Beijing or Shanghai. Many students were so poor that they had never traveled outside of Anhui Province, and they dreamed about foreign and domestic travel. Of course, I provided a living example of someone who had traveled widely, and consequently, I was a role model for their dreams.

For Robert, as had other foreigners before me, I provided guidance for his searching mind because, like him, I did not hold a normal perspective on life. So, we had a deep bond together in our viewpoint that there is more to life than just making money. At first, I think Robert had hoped that I shared his Christian beliefs, but my spiritual views provided enough scope that he could share his dreams with me. I tried to share my life experience with him, so that he could have a balanced viewpoint about life. Hopefully, I was a mentor for him, as he was a guide in China for me.

On a weekend foray, we went to Fengyang, a city that is only about a half of an hour bus ride from Bengbu. Fengyang had been one of the centers of the Ming Dynasty in the 14th century. As we walked through the center of the city, I was impressed at how old the city seemed to me. I thought to myself that this was what China must have been like in the past. In the middle of the city square stands a huge, imposing building called *"The Drum Tower,"* which was built by one of the Ming Dynasty emperors. It dominates the city square with a massive presence—it gives a rare glimpse into those times.

Robert took me to visit a famous Chinese painter whose shop is near the Drum Tower. The artist paints exquisite scenes inspired by those long ago times in the Ming Dynasty: phoenixes, beautiful Chinese women, and rural scenes. While we were in the shop, the artist took pictures with us. He was so happy to meet a foreigner who loved his art.

We then took a bus into the countryside outside of Fengyang, where there is an ancient Ming Dynasty tomb. We thought that the tomb we were visiting was a Ming emperor's tomb, but it was actually the tomb of his parents. Still, it was a beautiful place with large statues of Ming soldiers, courtiers, lions, rams, and horses lining the approach to the tombs. It was definitely like going back in time to the regal atmosphere of the Ming.

On another journey to Fengyang, we went to a cave that was about an hour bus ride outside of the city. I loved this area because it actually had forests and mountains large enough to be called mountains. The buildings around the cave were very old, and I had the feeling that

I had gone back in time to the 18th century. When we exited the bus, I saw a small house, which doubled as a restaurant. Most houses of this type in China are open to the outside, and I could see what looked like a menagerie of dead animals in piles on the floor: a small deer the size of a large dog, badgers, rabbits, and ducks. It was a poacher's paradise, but it was apparently legal in this area for the locals to have an open season. The hunter had obviously killed as many animals as possible. As I stood there, men came to buy the animals for their dinners. It was a booming business. An ancient woman approached me with a basket full of herbs, mushrooms, and tea that she had picked on the mountain. I had my friend tell her that I would buy some when I returned.

The cave was a huge limestone formation, which had been used by the Chinese military in their fight against the Japanese during *World War Two*. There were many large rooms with stalactites and stalagmites in fanciful formations everywhere. What made the cave extraordinarily beautiful was that, unlike in America where an effort is made to keep things as natural as possible, the Chinese want to make things as beautiful as possible. Throughout the cave, multi-colored lights had been arranged behind formations in each room that were activated by noise, such as clapping your hands. So, each cavernous room was illuminated with these technicolor lights—it was a fantasy land of great beauty. I had fantasies of becoming a troglodyte living in the cave far from the modern world.

My life at Bengbu College would have been impossible without Robert's conscientious effort to invite me each Sunday for some new adventure. So many people asked for my phone number or said that they wanted to be my friend, but Robert is the only person who followed through, and made my time in China less lonely. It was wonderful to have a friend who helped me to acclimate to a foreign culture and who shared his heart with me. I will be forever grateful for his friendship.

"Leave Him Alone"

After the first two weeks of September, I had very little contact with the Bengbu College administration or the foreign language department. I would see my advisor, Derrick, every week for a brief meeting, but this was usually the only interaction that I would have. On about the third week of September, I was notified that several people from the foreign language department would be observing one of my classes. Five people from the department came to the class on that day, including the head of the department and a few teachers. A teacher had asked me if I would be nervous when they came, but I said—"No, I was confident in my teaching capabilities."

And, indeed, on the day that they came, I had fun because it was a music class in which I played a few songs, and then the students had to tell me the meaning of the English lyrics. The two songs I chose that day, "Viva La Vida" by Coldplay and "Keep Me in Your Heart" by Warren Zevon, were well received by the students and by the other teachers. I noticed that the other teachers were trying to figure out the meaning of the lyrics, and nodded their heads when they had guessed correctly that the Zevon song was about his imminent death. I never received any reaction to the class from the department other than that I should include some lessons from the textbook during the class. I had not received the textbook until two weeks into the first semester, and had not included it into the lesson plan at that point.

From that point on, I rarely, if ever, saw the contact teachers, Ms. Zhao and Mr. Wong, and I began to wonder if I'd had halitosis or American B.O.. I knew that the foreign language department had regular meetings with all the Chinese teachers, but I was never invited. In fact, I was never formally introduced to any of the

Chinese teachers who taught in English in the department, outside of these two contact teachers. I really wondered about this, but I just thought that everyone was too busy. I didn't talk to the head of the department, Mr. Wu, again until the final exams in December. I was on my own to devise my lesson plans and to teach the students, which I was completely fine with, because I knew the focus of what I wanted to teach the students.

Then, one day, I was eating my dinner in the dining room, when a young man came to my table and said hello. At first, I thought he was a student, but after about five minutes, I realized that he was a fellow English teacher. We chatted about the students, whom he felt were really hopeless in their abilities to learn English. He was more than pessimistic about their scholastic abilities. And then he said it! He told me that at a meeting of all the English teachers, the department chairman, Mr. Wu, when he was discussing my presence at the college told them to, "Leave him alone." It was at that point that I realized that, no, I didn't have American B.O., but rather all of the teachers had been directed to give me space, and not to interfere with my being at the college. All the teachers were just following a department policy concerning foreign teachers. It was clear that the department head felt that if all the teachers tried to interact with me, I would be overwhelmed.

Although this might have been true on some levels, I would have enjoyed interactions with other professionals, particularly with those who spoke English, but I was relegated to being unapproachable by the department's directive. Before coming to China, I had visions of having many Chinese friends, especially other teachers, with whom I would have dinner and socialize. Unfortunately, this was not to be, and I was left alone. The friendships that I was to develop during my time in China were to be among the students, and this took a long time to develop because of their natural shyness. As a result, the cold months came to China without my having a group of friends. I was alone.

Solitude and Her Sisters

The last days of October, 2009, were hot in the 80's Fahrenheit, but then overnight, the temperature fell to only the 30's—winter-like weather had come to stay in Bengbu. When I went into the city center that week, I noticed in the shopping area that workers around large trucks were unloading large bundles of winter coats, quilts, and sweaters. That was when I realized that winter in this part of China is not warm. Yes, "Old Man Winter" was to be a constant visitor to Anhui Province in the next months.

One morning, I was exiting the north gate of the campus, when I noticed a woman in a long white medical coat, standing at the entrance. As lines of students would approach, she would press a metal looking instrument to their heads, and then direct them forward through the gate, or with some, into the police building at the gate. Well, this got my American mind into an apprehensive dither! I was confused and did not know what the instrument the woman was using could possibly be!? That was when I realized that it must have something to do with the H1NI flu virus epidemic sweeping the world. I definitely did not want her putting that device to my head! My American belief in privacy, and against government intrusion into our lives, reared its head and I thought to myself—"She's not going to use that thing on me!" The Chinese students, however, sheep-like, followed her directions without hesitation. Finally, not having any choice as to whether I had wanted to get out of the gate, I allowed her to examine me with her device; and as she waved me through the gate, I said, *"Zai-jien"* (goodbye).

That next week, I was standing outside of the classroom during a break, when Mr. Wong came over to talk to me. I asked him what the device was that the woman doctor was using at the gate. He laughed and explained to me that it was a thermometer that the Chinese had developed during the SARS epidemic a few years earlier. He told me that there was a lot of apprehension about the swine flu outbreak in China, and that any student who'd had a fever was being quarantined for possibly having the flu! I told him how different China was when compared to America, and how such a public examination be unthinkable in America. He agreed with me. China is really a different world!

Then Derrick, my advisor, told me that all large student gatherings were being prohibited due to the swine flu. Unfortunately, that meant that the English Corner Association gatherings were now canceled. So much for my short run as a rock star!

With the coming of the winter weather and the swine flu, my Chinese world became restricted. Solitude and her sisters: loneliness, illness, and despair, had come to Bengbu College. The isolation of this period was heightened by the shortness of the days, as night would come by 5 p.m., and it would be dark long before the end of the teaching day at 6 p.m.

At the same time, the students retreated into their dormitories from the cold. There were no students hanging out at the basketball courts or on the playgrounds. Everyone was huddling inside, trying to stay warm. That was when I found out something that was incomprehensible to me as an American. The students' dormitory rooms did not have heat. I could not believe it! The students told me that when it got cold, they would get under their quilts in their beds, or sometimes if it got really cold they would sleep in the same beds. They told me that with six people in a dorm room, it was warm enough. Then I noticed that all of their dorm windows were open even on the coldest days! Yes, the students would leave their windows open during the day, even when it was in the 20's Fahrenheit. They were simply used to the cold weather for some reason.

Then, one day I was looking at the roofs on the houses in the neighboring villages, and realized that there were no chimneys on any of the roofs. Then to my amazement, I understood why the students had their windows open: no one has heat in the whole Anhui Province. None of the small brick homes in the villages had heat. When I would ride by on my bicycle during the day, the doors to the small houses would be open, and people would be sitting outside in the sunshine if it had happened to be sunny. People in this part of China live without heat of any kind. So, that was why the students did not close their windows. They too were used to the cold weather!

The most bizarre feature of this winter dream was that the classrooms in the college did not have heat either! I had heard about this bizarre way of education—"refrigerator classrooms"—before I came to China; but I did not fully realize what that meant. The students and yes, yours truly, would wear winter coats, hats, and gloves in the classroom! Not only did the classrooms not have any heat; often they were colder than the outside, because no sunshine had reached many of the classrooms to warm them up. It was like teaching in an icebox! Some students would bring these little hand warmers, which were filled with water that they could plug into an electric socket to heat them up. I felt like Frosty the Snowman with my many layers of clothing and a coat, including long underwear, teaching the students. Frosty, unfortunately, was not as acclimated as the Chinese students to the winter in Anhui Province. Eight hours of classes in a sub-freezing classroom was a physical as well as an intellectual challenge. The students, to their credit, were braver than their American teacher.

The other strange feature in the classroom during these cold days was that many of the female students wore masks. Students started wearing masks as the weather became colder, and then colder; although some people were wearing masks even in October because of their fear of the flu. So, as I looked out over my classroom, I saw a group of masked bandits. Imagine trying to communicate in English with a student who naturally spoke very quietly, and who now was wearing a mask! Not only would the women students wear masks, but they would wear masks that were color-coordinated with their outfits. Color-coordinated bandits! The mask-wearing phenomenon was not just feminine, as even some men wore masks in the cold. I always thought to myself—what good do masks do?

I had to immediately go into Bengbu city to try to find a size 10 and a half boot, because my dress shoes would leave my precious feet frozen by the end of a teaching day. Of course, the task of finding that boot size in a world of small Chinese feet was a monumental undertaking. After going to many shoe stores, and many shopkeepers—who could only pantomime that they were sorry—I realized that I was not going to find my boot size by myself. I enlisted the services of my student friend, Robert, and went to a large department store in Bengbu, where we were able to find boots for my American-sized feet.

The Chinese students, however, were more prepared. The women all suddenly appeared in their ankle-high black boots and multi-colored pastel coats. The men all wore black coats with tennis shoes. It was the Chinese student winter uniform. Everyone looked alike in their winter gear. The women were the peacocks of the race and the men the sartorial "ugly ducklings". Somehow, we all managed to survive days and days in the ice-box classrooms with our frozen breath, hands, and feet.

Sister solitude was in full control of the campus, and would reign with her icy sisters till the semester ended in January. Her control on the college was emphasized one evening at the dining hall. The dining halls were also not immune to the cold. There was no heat there either, but rather the doors were open to the outside except for some slatted plastic that served as a barrier to the outside. So, it was frigid in the cafeteria as the students and I would eat our meals. Coats and hats were *de rigeur*!

As I was eating my dinner with a student, a fight broke out among the students near us. Five students were hitting and kicking another male student, not just hitting, but hitting with great force so as to do as much damage as possible. The student was bleeding from cuts on his face. The fight happened so quickly that I was surprised at its violence and unexpectedness. It had ended as fast as it had started, when the student broke away from the mob hitting him. This altercation was extremely unusual, and I only saw one other shoving match during the whole time that I was in China. I'm sure the cold and damp weather exacerbated the situation and influenced the students' behavior. Later, I asked a student about the fight. He told me that, if they had been caught in their brief rumble, all of the students involved in it would have been expelled.

The fight was the prelude to the next days, in which I became very ill. I had really bad diarrhea, but no fever, and, so, I knew it was not the flu. I stayed in bed for four days trying to feel better. I ate some noodle soup from "the cup of soup" type packaging in which you simply pour in hot water. I was afraid to eat the food from the dining hall because it was so spicy, which would not have been good for my American intestines. One day, I finally tried to call Robert to have him bring me some bland food, but I could not reach him. I was afraid to call my advisor, Derrick, for fear that they would say that I'd had the flu and that they would quarantine me. The experience of being ill in a foreign country by yourself is one of the real nightmares of life. I felt completely helpless. Fortunately, after those four days, the symptoms abated, and I was able to resume life. The diarrhea happened during my off days from school, so that I did not miss class; but I was afraid that, on the first day that I had returned to the classroom, that I would have to run for the squat toilets in the students' bathroom.

Many students were sick during this time too. Everyone had colds, pneumonia, or the flu. As a result, there were many absences from my classroom. I could not imagine what it must have been like in the dormitories with no heat, and to be ill with a fever also. The students, however, bravely faced all difficulties including illness and lack of heat.

November and December were the greatest challenges during my stay in China. The cold, the darkness, illness, and the solitude—all of her sisters made my life a challenge. For me, the camaraderie with the students, the weekly adventures with Robert, the phone calls and Skype calls to my friends in America, were the means for surviving Solitude's sisters and the vicissitudes of the cold. Although I was a "stranger in a strange land," I was able to maintain my sanity with modern technology and the students' positive attitudes.

Oovoo, Skype, and Technology

What really saved me during the cold winter months, when Sister Solitude stalked the campus, was my computer and the Internet. Although I was physically thousands of miles away from friends and family, I was able to communicate with them on a daily basis using Skype or Oovoo. Skype is the Internet technology, which allows a person to call and to see their friends over the Internet. What is Oovoo? Oovoo is an Internet communication system, which enables a group of people to have a conference call and to see each other over the Internet. Each person on the computer screen is seen in a square, and everyone can talk to each other. Every day I would use these systems to talk to my friends and family. I know that, without being able to talk to the people I knew, I would have been put into the Chinese equivalent of the Oregon State Hospital for mental patients. During my time in China, I was linked with all of my friends through modern technology. Thank you, Internet!

I would get up each morning, and when the icon on my computer screen showed that a friend was online, I would call them and chat. This support system was essential in my Chinese world, where I had no friends. I became a 'netizen'—a citizen of the Internet. This was surprising to me, because normally I am an active person, who loves hiking and physical activity. My life and world revolved around my computer screen. It was more than an addiction—it was my lifeline to the world. During my stay in China, there were a few days when the Internet was down. I would become very anxious, almost frantic about being able to communicate with the world again. Although the Internet became a surrogate reality for me, the tangible connection that it provided was essential to my mental health.

Before I came to China, I was very concerned about my ability to find books and movies in English. I knew from my previous trips to China that there simply were not many books available in English. My life had always revolved around reading books and watching movies, and I was worried that I would not have this entertainment anymore. What I did not know was that all of this is available for free on the Internet.

My advisor, Derrick, told me that there was a collection of English books on the sixth floor of the library, but when I went there to check it out, I found out what English books were available. Old scientific and mathematics textbooks! Yes, there were two rooms filled with ancient textbooks! I was able to find a couple of books that were interesting to me, but I knew that I was really in trouble—as far as reading was concerned, if this was all that was available.

Then I went on the Internet, and did a search for what was available. I had heard that there were projects being implemented to turn university libraries into online libraries of e-books. I was overjoyed to discover that, indeed, there were many library resources available online. The ones that I used were from *The Gutenberg Project,* which is the largest online library on the Internet, but this resource had primarily books that had been published before the 1920's. Then I found *Burgomeister's Books,* which is a website with more current titles that are available to be downloaded. So, during my time in China, I was able to read many novels and nonfiction works that were in online libraries.

The other entertainment that I really enjoy is watching movies. I was not sure before coming to China what English movies would be available. I did not think there would be many video stores. What I discovered was truly amazing! There were many websites online, with every movie that a movie addict like me could possibly desire. These websites allow you to click on a link with downloaded movies from everywhere. Some links to movies would play very well and others would not, but usually you could watch any movie that you had wanted. The websites had all of the current movies such as *Avatar*, *District 9*, *The Hurt Locker*, *Up in the Air*, and everything else. Also, all of the older movies could be watched too! I was in heaven. So, many nights in China were consumed watching movies online. My favorite websites were *Watch Movies Online TV* and *Youkou*.

Then, there was music. With the Internet, I could listen to my local National Public Radio station, Jefferson Public Radio, from Ashland, Oregon, streaming on the cybernetic airwaves. Then, there are many websites with radio stations of every genre from around the world. My favorite, though, was *Grooveshark,* a music website that allows you to create playlists of all of your favorite music—I would simply input which song I wanted to hear, and create playlists based on my selection. I would also download music from Chinese websites that I would play in the classroom for the students.

If I wanted news, there were so many websites that provided me with American or international news. My favorite new site was *Reference Desk.com,* which is a resource with every conceivable newspaper, encyclopedia, dictionary, and other reference-related information. As a diversion, and on a daily basis, I went to this website to find out what was going on in the world.

Thanks to modern technology, the Internet helped me to stay in touch with friends…and provided me with a world of entertainment that I did not know about before coming to China. In some ways, I was more connected to the world at that time than before I had gone abroad. For expatriates, the Internet is our lifeline. There is the frustration that the Chinese government has blocked many websites available in the West, but for me this was a minor hindrance to a magical world inside of the magic box, which was my computer.

Silent Night

The darkness of this time before the winter solstice is always a challenge for me, but in China I was living in an internal, isolated world such as I had never experienced. I would teach my classes, and return to my apartment for an evening of watching movies or surfing the Internet. I bought some Christmas lights, and strung them around my living room to bring in some holiday cheer. I lit candles in an effort to bring more light into my life.

As Christmas approached, my students asked me what I was doing for the holiday. I told them that I was just going to spend a quiet day at home. When I asked them how, or if Christmas was celebrated in China, they told me that some people give gifts and have parties. They told me that each class of students usually had parties. Christmas is not celebrated as a formal holiday, but many people celebrate it themselves in a very festive way. New Year's Day, however, is a formal holiday.

As the magic day approached, the students told me about their parties and invited me to attend. Of course, I was happy to attend as many as I could before the actual holiday. I had a great time at many of these parties. The students provided refreshments, candy, and nuts to eat. Students provided entertainment by singing songs, performing skits, or by having a session of karaoke. Of course, I was asked to perform and, at one of them, I gave a heartfelt rendition of 'Silent Night," which was well received. Many students told me that they had never heard the Christmas carol before.

As I was guided home by the students from one party, we were accompanied by two Chinese English teachers who lived in the same apartment building as I had been living. I had never met them before. They shared the same apartment a few doors down from me. One of them had asked me if I had heat. I said, "Of course, an

American could never live without heat!" She looked at me with some angst and said, "We don't. The college told us that it was too expensive!" I felt ashamed, when I realized that even my fellow teachers had no heat in the frigid weather. I was ashamed that I was being treated differently, because I was an American.

One night, there was a festive gathering sponsored by the English Corner Association with hundreds of students in attendance. I was the guest of honor. Again the evening consisted of many performers singing songs, skits, conducting funny activities, and spreading laughter throughout the air. I was the honored guest. When I stood to sing before the assemblage of students, I decided to give them a Christmas blessing by singing the old song, "May the Long Time Sun Shine Upon You." The students loved it! Of course, I was a rock star again—photographs, and many conversations followed. It really was a joyous gathering. As I walked home, I saw many orange Chinese lanterns flying high in the sky.

Just before Christmas, the college had a feast for me at a fancy restaurant in Bengbu—another 'Kembay' evening with many alcoholic toasts. All of the college administration was there. I sat next to Number One and had a wonderful time, between toasts, talking about foreign travel. I was given several Christmas presents by other teachers and from the college. Like an American, I opened the presents there, which I found out later on that you are not supposed to do in China. The excepted practice for Chinese people is that when you are given a gift, you wait until later when you are by yourself to open the gifts. I had much to learn about China. It was a pleasant evening and I felt very grateful for the kindness of everyone towards me.

After the dinner, I was taken by car to downtown Bengbu to see the festivities there. There were huge crowds of people everywhere. Some were standing on street corners where stages had been set up and where people were entertaining the crowds by singing. Crowds of people were in the stores buying Christmas presents. Christmas lights were shining on many buildings, and storefronts were decorated with Christmas decorations. Sales clerks were dressed in Santa hats, and Saint Nick himself made an appearance! I found out that Christmas as a holiday is alive and well in China!

The hallowed day itself was an anti-climax, as I'd had several classes to teach that day. The students expressed dismay over the reality that they had to attend classes on Christmas, but what could we do? After classes that night, I watched a movie, and was thankful that I had survived my first semester as an English teacher in China.

A Cold North Wind

When I would walk to classes every day, I would cross the square in front of the library, and look up to see which way the red Chinese flag was blowing on that day. Invariably, in the winter, the flag was blowing straight out to the south, indicating a brisk wind from the north. Brisk would be an understatement because this cold north wind blew straight out of Mongolia for months.

The official Anhui government website describes the weather there as "in the transitional area between [the] temperate zone and subtropical zone, so the climate there is warm and moist, and the four seasons are distinct." The government website goes on to say that Anhui has a moist, monsoon climate with the temperature ranging from 14 degrees Centigrade to 17 degrees Centigrade. Not to disagree with the government, but I want to tell you that northern Anhui Province is a damn cold place!

From November to May, I almost always wore long underwear and wool socks, especially when I was in the classrooms. My winter coat became a permanent part of my body, and I felt like I had lived and slept in the garment. The wind would blow so hard that I was thankful that my coat had protected me from the vicious blasts. Women from the villages wore quilted pajama as outfits around town, which looked really warm, even if they had appeared as though they had just gotten out of bed. And what always astonished me was that the young men on campus never wore hats even in the coldest weather. I guessed that maybe their hair was some kind of new hat apparel, and that I wasn't really seeing correctly. At least, the young women had the sense to dress for winter with hats, gloves, boots, winter coats and masks.

Another thing that had surprised me was that there was very little moisture of any kind during the winter. It had rained a few times, and snowed maybe four times; but the precipitation really was not very significant. The deepest snow that fell was about six inches high. It was just always cold and windy, with normally slate-gray skies. Not really a place for a person who might have a seasonal affective disorder.

I was truly thankful for the two heating systems located in my bedroom and office. I spent most of my time that winter huddled in my office, with the door closed to maintain the heat. I had two warm quilts on my bed, which prevented me from turning into an ice block by morning. Having had my heating installed did make me feel guilty over the reality that no one else had any heat on campus, but I knew that I could never live in such a climate without it. Americans are just plain spoiled—that's the truth.

I was so glad at the first signs of spring, which began in March; but really it did not get constantly warm until May. It was six months of winter, with a cold north wind for my Oregon blood, but thanks to the heat in my apartment, I survived without any frostbite.

A Big Red Ball

In mid-December, I gave all of my five hundred students their final examinations, which were comprised primarily of grammar questions. This was an examination that I had written, based on the grammar lessons that I had taught the students during the semester. Some of the exam sessions had up to a hundred students in one room taking the exam, which presented space problems, because the students were sitting next to each other. Even though I had warned them not to talk to each other, and not to look at each other's examinations, I was surprised that many of them did it anyway. I had to warn them many times not to cheat. I told them that if they had done that in America, they would be excused from the classroom and be given a failing mark. In my opinion, the students were just going about business as usual, talking with each other in their collective way— who cared if it was a final examination?! I told them again, that in America, when someone was caught cheating, they would be asked to leave and be given a failing grade. The physical setting of the examinations almost facilitated cheating. After the week-long examination period, I had five hundred examinations to grade over the course of a few weeks. I figured with one hundred answers for each test and five hundred students, I had close to fifty thousand responses to grade. It was a physical challenge for my eyes just to complete the task.

Although New Year's Day is a holiday in China, it is not celebrated in the same way as in the West, because the real New Year comes at the Chinese New Year, which in 2009, was celebrated in February. There were a few more fireworks than normally, but otherwise, the holiday was uneventful. So, I continued to grade final examinations during the first two weeks of January, while trying to do a certain portion each day and not to go crazy in seeing the same answers five hundred times. Chinese students give themselves English names, because the foreign teachers, including me, cannot pronounce or remember their Chinese names. These are often fanciful names such as Pink, Gray, Happy, or Sunny. So, I had to be careful—after I had graded the examinations—to mark the proper grade next to their English and Chinese names, along with the student number. It took me two weeks, or up until mid-January, before I had completed my monumental task; but I was so happy when I turned the grades in to the English department head. I had completed my first semester as an English teacher in China.

During the month of January, the greatest blessing that came was the clarity of winter—clear skies and cold temperatures. I was so happy to see the blue sky and that clear light, which is typical of January in the northern hemisphere. Every evening the sun would set like a big red ball caught in the hand of the night. Nowhere else in the world have I experienced this phenomenon—the sun as a giant red being on the Chinese western horizon. After months of dirty, gray weather, I found such peace in the blue skies and in the wonderful sunsets.

At the same time, since there were no classes, I was substantially alone for several weeks. When the students had finished their final examinations, they departed for their homes all over the Anhui Province. In China, there is a break between the winter and spring semesters, which lasts from mid-January until March 1st. It is during this time that the Chinese New Year—and the other major holiday of China, the Spring Festival—were to take place.

I had to devise a routine to keep myself busy in the solitude. Each day I would work on lesson plans to prepare for the spring semester. This was a significant task, because I would be teaching two curriculums then. So, I had to prepare coursework for two different types of classes. I also had to spend a lot of time exercising:

taking walks, doing yoga, and riding my bike despite the cold. One day, I was talking to a friend about my routine. She said, "That is a lot like being in prison." When I thought about it, I realized that that was what people do in prison.

The other problem that I'd had during this time was that the lunchroom had closed at the end of January, which meant that I had to cook my own meals. So, I had to take the bus into Bengbu, shop at the Carrefour, the major grocery store, take a taxi home, and cook my meals. It was much more expensive than the cheap meals that I could eat at the cafeteria....Not to mention, also, that I was subject to the simplicity of my limited cooking skills. But I was able to make simple, nutritious meals.

I was preparing to travel to Jiuhuashan, which is a mountainous area in the southern Anhui Province known as being one of the four sacred Buddhist mountains in China. I had to prepare myself to make the journey, because I was going to stay there for three weeks in February. It was to be a magical and blessed journey.

Jiuhuashan Beauty

The Spring Festival—like the Autumn Festival—is one of the main holidays in China which lasts a whole week, during which time all Chinese people travel to be with their families. It is a combination of Christmas and Thanksgiving: big feasts are celebrated with dumplings being one of the main courses. My students kept asking me where I was going to spend the holiday. When I told them that I was going to Jiuhuashan by myself, they stared at me in silent disbelief; because for Chinese people, being by yourself during the Spring Festival, is incomprehensible.

Jiuhuashan is one of the four sacred Buddhist mountains in China. It is located in southern Anhui Province quite near the famed Huangshan or Yellow Mountain. Jiuhuashan, which means "Nine Jeweled Mountains" for its nine prominent peaks, has been an area sacred to Buddhists for many centuries. In 719 Kim Gio Gak, a member of one of Korea's royal families, came to Jiuhuashan to live in a cave in search of enlightenment. Known as the "Cave Dwelling Monk," he died when he was ninety-nine years old, and was proclaimed to be the Ksitigarbha Boddhisattva, who was dedicated to helping all souls attain enlightenment.

Thereafter, temple building began, and continued from the Song Dynasty until the Qing Dynasty. Today there are seventy-three ancient temples, with over 6,300 Buddhist statues in Jiuhuashan. There is a legend that the Sakyamuni Buddha preached in the garden of the Qiyuan Temple for twenty years. In the Longevity Palace, located on the top of a peak above the village, is the gilded mummy of Wu Xia, who was a holy monk who lived on the mountain from 1573-1619. Wu Xia copied eighty-one volumes of Buddhist scriptures, using blood from his tongue and gold powder. When he died at the advanced age of over one hundred years, his fellow monks gilded his corpse because of his sanctity. At the top of one of the peaks is the Tiantai Temple, where Buddhists climb to the summit of heaven to worship.

After changing buses in Hefei, my journey from Bengbu took about seven hours until I had arrived in Jiuhuashan. As a person who lives in and loves mountains, I was overjoyed to see the mountains appear as we headed southward. We crossed the Yangtze River, which is the largest river in China—and in my mind, I could imagine all of the ships journeying down the river to the sea. After the bus came to a large city, a family on the bus got off along the road, and the driver motioned me to join them. Thinking that maybe this was where I was to get off, I joined them along the side of the road. Soon, it became apparent that they were going to give me a ride up the mountain in their car. They were a family from Shanghai who were eager to meet an American. As we proceeded up the mountain, light snow was falling on the pine trees. By the time they had dropped me at my hotel in the center of the village, the ground was covered with an inch of snow.

The Dragon Springs Hotel was located in the heart of the village, with many monasteries and temples situated along the main road through town. In fact, there was a monastery next to the hotel, and in the morning I could hear the clack, clack, clack as a percussion instrument called the monks to morning prayer and meditation at 4:30 a.m. I loved to hear this sound every morning, and then again in the afternoon. Somehow, I felt as if I were participating in the monks' worship and daily life. I was on my own three-week retreat in the mountains.

That first afternoon, I explored all of the temples along the main road. It was hard to count the number of temples, but there seemed to be a temple on every hill and along the entire street. Shops selling Buddhist souvenirs also lined the street. People shouted out *"laowai"* or yelled hello to me as I walked around. The smell of incense wafted in the air, and with the snow, was beyond magical. Some of the temples had statues of the Buddha in them that were as big as houses. I was awestruck by the grandeur and holiness of the town. I heard bells gonging and monks chanting all along the street.

That evening I had my first meal of many at the hotel restaurant. I was happy because the restaurant had an English menu, but even with the translation, I did not know what most of the dinners on the menu were. There followed a nightly performance. I would point to an item, say to "Pockmarked Grandma's Tofu," and the waitress would go and ask the cook if they had the meal. She would soon return to tell me that it was not available. I would laugh, and go down the list with the same result. Finally, I would usually choose the one item that I knew they would have, and which I liked: "Kung Pao Chicken." This would always bring howls of laughter that the *"laowai"* always picked the same thing. It was a *"laowai"* dinner!

The next day, I climbed the thousands of steps to the "Longevity Palace," and to the pavilion located on the ridge above town. By the time I had reached the top, I knew that I had done some exercise! My muscles were like lead after the workout, but how glorious it was to see the temples. They were ancient with several large Buddhas in each major temple; but it was so foggy that I could not see them at first, being guided through the temple solely by the lighted candles inside. I walked everywhere in the Longevity Palace, but I could not find Wu Xia's mummy. The sight of the snow-covered pavilion, several stories high, was like something from a Ming Dynasty dream.

That afternoon, the skies cleared, and I could see the ridgeline above town with its temples and the pavilion guarding the town. I realized that I was really in a magical place, such as what I had imagined China would be when

I had been younger. There were many monks and nuns walking along the main street of the village, and I realized that Jiuhuashan was still a very active Buddhist center.

On the third day, I climbed to the top of the ridge above town, and then continued on the other side down the mountain, where I found a small hut. Inside, a small nun dressed in acorn brown beckoned me inside. She offered me some rice and vegetables, and cleaned off some chopsticks with an oily black rag for my use. As we sat together eating, I realized that the hut was really a small temple, with three small golden Buddhas. My nun friend was the guardian of the temple. After the simple meal, I made my obeisance and continued along the stone stairway.

After I had descended the mountain, I crossed a bridge over a large stream with giant boulders. On the other side was a nunnery with its golden walls, temples, and many Buddhas. Beyond the nunnery was the upper village with "The Phoenix Pine," a tree said to be fourteen hundred years old. Above the village, Tiantai Mountain rose up into heaven, and I could see many temples stretched along the way from top to bottom.

I had found the proverbial "stairway to heaven" with its many Buddhist temples. The challenge for the worshipper is to ascend what seems like a million steps to the top, where Tiantai Temple resides, well beyond the pale of the world. My legs were talking to me as I made my ascent, but the scenery was legendary in its grandeur: misshapen rocks, waterfalls, streams, and pine trees clinging to the stony ledges. As I climbed the mountain, I stopped at each temple to bow before the Buddhas in residence there.

As I came past one temple, I suddenly saw a band of monkeys eating food thrown to them by tourists. These were not your ordinary small monkeys, but they had rather a cowl around their necks, and were each about the size of a large dog. They were unabashed to see me as they munched on their treats; but then I saw a group of babies clinging to the trees. They were more skittish, and would jump if I had approached too closely. So cute! I love monkeys, and I was so happy to have found the monkey paradise.

I journeyed onward up the mountain, going from temple to temple. I couldn't help but think that this was what I had always dreamed of doing when I was a young man— to just spend the day walking in the mountains among the temples. I really didn't want to return to the village that I could see so far below, but my legs were aching, and I thought that I had reached the top. I was to learn on another climb that Tiantai Temple was actually just above where I had stopped.

On the following day, my legs were so tight that I could only climb above Qiyuan Temple in the snow to the Quan Yin Cave where I had tea with the monks. I tried to follow the signs up the stone stairs to "The Tiger Cave," but I was not able to find it that day. I decided I had better rest my legs for another day.

Thereafter, almost every day I would follow the same path up the mountains and the stairway to heaven to the temples. I finally made it to the top where Tiantai Temple reigns in its lofty ether. On my way, I stopped to see my nun friend, and we sang chants to Amithaba Buddha. I was always happy to get my tired legs back to my hotel room to rest.

Then the magic day of the Chinese New Year came. I had discovered the center of the village behind the hotel, where there is a large central square bordered by shops, and a giant pond in the middle filled with golden fish. I noticed that all of the shopkeepers were closing their stores and taping red banners on their doors, which I found out said things like: wealth, prosperity, happiness, and good health. By the afternoon, it had started snowing—and it was a dream-world of deep white, as snow covered the temples. I was resting in my room, when I heard dissonant-sounding music coming from the monastery next door. I looked out of the window, and saw a candle-lit dragon of about twenty-feet long, with many people's legs sticking out from below. A band was playing music as the dragon danced by the monastery. The dragon sauntered by my window, as I tried to take pictures of its illuminated coils. I ran outside and followed it down the street in the falling snow.

The streets were filled with thousands of people who had come from all over China to celebrate the New Year and to worship at the temples. Fireworks exploded everywhere: skyrockets, firecrackers, and noise-makers of every kind. It was like the whole world was exploding in delight! The revelry and merriment of the people was infectious. I saw many other dragons, going from shop to shop, to bring them good luck for the New Year. Meanwhile, I was in ecstasy from the celebration, but at the same time, I was trying not to get blown up by the many fireworks exploding around me. Then fireworks started skyrocketing from the mountaintops, as people at the temples joined the display. I thought to myself how wonderful it was to have lived to see a real Chinese New Year.

When I returned to my hotel room to try and sleep, I realized that that was not going to be easy on this night of revelry. The fireworks continued without abatement for the whole night and through until the next afternoon, when the exhausted people must have finally sat down to New Year's feasts. It was the biggest celebration that I had ever seen. The Chinese really know how to celebrate a holiday!

In the following days, Jiuhuashan was crowded with thousands of Buddhist worshippers. After the big snow, I climbed up the stairway to heaven, but took a detour away from the throng on the stairways. I reached an area atop of the mountain, away from Tiantai Temple, with a view of all of the mountains extending out to infinity. It was warm and the sun was hot on my face even with all of the snow. I made my way back to the temple along the ridge. There were so many people on the ice-covered stairway below the temple that I prayed that I would make it past the crowd without falling. I did fall once, but luckily did not hurt myself on the steps. I knew then that it was too dangerous to climb the mountain, with all of the people and the snow.

So on the following day, I had determined to find "The Tiger Cave," where I knew that there would not be many people. I climbed up the steps, and then descended to the other side of the mountain where I was greeted with a spectacular view of the Nine Jeweled Mountains against the blue sky. As soon as I saw the Tiger Cave, I knew that I was in a sacred place. The door to the cave was locked and I could not get inside, but there was no one there. I sat outside of the door in the sunshine for an hour, absorbing the peace and solitude. Then, a monk from the little house near the cave motioned for me to join him. When I went into the house, two nuns were sitting, watching, and listening to a Buddhist video of monks chanting. They poured me tea, and I sat with them for an hour as they chatted with each other. It was so peaceful that I just wanted to stay and live with them in their simple shelter. Finally, I bid them adieu, and climbed back up the mountain. The Tiger Cave—a place of sacredness!

On my last day in Jiuhuashan, I climbed up the mountain for the last time to the Longevity Palace, hoping to finally pay my respects to Wu Xia. When I entered the temple, I bowed to the Buddha there, and then circumambulated around it to find a small room behind. There was Wu Xia in his golden glory! He looked like a sacred golden small man. I bowed my respects to his holiness and continued to another temple complex, whereafter I left a donation. The monks motioned me to climb some stairs. Up at the height of the stairs, I found a room filled with Five Hundred Arahats—five hundred life-like carved statues of Bodhisattvas, each with their own individual features and mudras. I was in awe at the feeling of sacredness. It was like being with the living presence of five hundred Buddhas. It was a sacred goodbye from the Buddhas of Jiuhuashan!

Diogenes and Friends

In March of 2010, I started the second semester of teaching at Bengbu College. Seven of the classes were to be advanced oral English classes. When I asked the head of the English department what I should focus on during the semester, he said, "Be creative." This gave me a *carte blanche* that would allow me to do what I had wanted!

In the first part of each class, I focused on some game or role-play to capture the attention of the students. The second part of the class involved grammar and a subject to talk about. The students had told me that they wanted to do more role-plays and to talk about America too. So I devised some different role-plays, involving both real life situations and also those which used famous characters.

What amazed me during the second semester was the transformation in the willingness of the students to talk. It was like I was interacting with a whole new group of students: I could not keep them quiet at times. In every class, my goal was to have every student to speak at least once, and hopefully more than that. The students now knew who I was, which gave them a comfort level to speak with me and to discuss issues that interested them. Many of my classes were large, with between forty to fifty students, which is really too much for an oral English class. What happened was that the students would talk at length about things, and it would be difficult for me to get them to keep their opinions brief, so as to allow other students to speak. Starting out as being shy, almost catatonically so, my students had now been infected with verbal diarrhea. I had created a monster!

Another major problem was the physical structure of the classroom itself. For oral English classes focused on role-plays and talking, it is optimal to have a seating arrangement that can be moved and reshaped. Unfortunately, the desks in the classrooms were arranged in rows and could not be moved. So, when it became time for the students to talk to each other in groups, a problem had been created by the fact that the seats could not be moved. Also, the large class size made it difficult to divide the students into groups for playing games.

The students loved to play games in which several teams would compete against each other in word games, such as *"Tongue Twisters"* or *"Dear Abby."* In the *Tongue Twisters* game students, divided into teams, would try to say very difficult tongue twisters such as the famous, "Peter Piper picked a peck of pickled peppers." I introduced the *Dear Abby* game by pretending to be an advice columnist such as the writer who had authored "Dear Abby," but Dear Michael, dressed up in a tie and wore sunglasses. In the *Dear Abby* game, four teams of students gave advice in response to real letters from the "Dear Abby" column; and the other students served as judges who would determine which student had given the best advice.

The role-plays were hugely popular with the students, who were given situational contexts in which to perform everyday sorts of actions, such as: a restaurant, a grocery store, an airport, a law court, or a school. They then had to devise a role-play within that setting, utilizing predetermined characters. The students had fun playing teachers and students, tourists, judges, store clerks, and restaurant customers. My favorite was the grocery store, a role-play in which the students had each pretended to be fruits and vegetables.

Sometimes, just getting the Chinese students to move away from their friends to form groups for the role-plays was the biggest problem. In my mind, it reemphasized the fact that Chinese students are a collective, and not a mix of individuals. Of course, in any country, students will not want to change seats and move away from friends, but the Chinese student reaction to the request to move was almost traumatic to them. At times, students would not move into new groups even when requested, and I would have to make repeated requests or wait for them to comply.

Another role-play was the *"Balloon Debate,"* in which students were divided into groups of four famous people who were in a hot air balloon together. Each student would role-play a famous person like: Madonna, Bruce Lee, Gong Li, or their favorite, Kobe Bryant. The situation they were given was that the hot air balloon had a leak, and there would be only enough air left to keep one person alive. So, the "famous people" had to debate each other in order to decide which of them would live, while the others had to jump out of the balloon. I dovetailed my own presence into this activity by playing King Solomon, the wise king, who helped the students to decide who was to live or die. I pretended to be King Solomon by wearing a shawl and a prayer hat! The students loved this role-play of bringing their favorite famous characters to life in the classroom—George Bush Jr., Chairman Mao, Barack Obama, Hillary Clinton, and Marilyn Monroe all made their appearances. If the famous person was a singer like Elvis Presley or John Lennon, I sang songs from their music with the students. We had so much fun! I had predicted to myself that the Chinese students would have their famous person voluntarily jump out of the balloon in self-sacrifice, because of the Chinese cultural value of placing the group ahead of the individual. I was exactly right as character after character volunteered to jump out of the balloon. I would then tell the famous person that it was going to be a long way down if they had decided to jump out, and I even demonstrated this fact by getting on top of the desks, and jumping! Of course, the students still wanted to have their famous person jump.

"Zodiac" was probably the favorite group activity for the students. In the *Zodiac* activity, the students were divided up into their sun signs: Capricorn, Taurus, Leo, and so

on. I then gave them a list of personal qualities attributed to that sun sign, and they had to pick two personal qualities that fit themselves, which they would then share with the whole class. I played the Greek philosopher, Diogenes, replete with a shawl over my head and a Diogenes lantern, my flashlight. The story is that, in broad daylight, Diogenes went into the marketplace of Athens with a lantern. When asked what he was doing, he said, "I am looking for an honest human being." I surprised the students so much when I walked around with my flashlight, peering at them and looking for a human being with my flashlight, that one student even jumped into the air in shock. The students loved this activity so much that they talked and talked about themselves and the qualities that they each had. It was impossible to contain their enthusiasm for the "zodiac," which contrasted with the Chinese astrological yearly calendar.

"Utopia" was another group activity that the students loved. I dressed up in a simulated toga with my shawl, as Plato, who introduced his book The Republic, which is about a utopia. Then the students, in groups of eight, formed a country to decide what laws, economy, political system, and rights their utopia would have. I prefigured that the students would base much of their laws on the actual laws in China, but some students were very creative in devising countries with national credit cards for all citizens, a future country where education would not be needed, because citizens would be implanted with a computer chip with all information—and many of their countries had "green economies."

The students were also intrigued when we discussed and compared Chinese and American cultural differences. Particularly interesting for them was what it was like for a Chinese student to live in America, and how the Chinese student found it impossible to integrate fully into the American culture. Many students had dreamt about going to an American university for graduate school, but they were surprised to find out how expensive that would be. Overall, I was pleased that the students were very forthright in wanting to talk about so many things during the last semester. Diogenes and his friends, even though they had come from far away in time and space, were effective cheerleaders in sparking interesting discussions in the classroom.

"The Heart Is an Organ of Fire"

For two of my classes, which had hosted the most advanced students in their oral English language ability, we read and discussed the novels, <u>The English Patient</u> by Michael Ondaatje, and <u>Cold Mountain</u> by Charles Frazier. I had chosen these two novels, because I wanted my students to read two modern novels that I had considered to be literary masterpieces. Most Chinese students had only read classical English literature, and so, I had felt that this would give them an insight into modern literature. At the same time, I felt that they would learn new English vocabulary, and learn a lot about life, love, and themselves. My premise was that, although I thought it would be very challenging for them to read these books, the novels would present excellent discussion topics for the classroom, increase their vocabulary, and inspire them with the great beauty of the written language.

In fact, the books were too difficult for most of the students to read, but I felt that the discussions in the classroom filled in the gaps in the plots. The issues, presented in both novels, intrigued the students—especially the beautiful love stories. I have always been inspired by the beauty of the English language; and both novels offered a myriad of new words for the students to learn. Each class was divided into three sections: in the first part of the class, we discussed the storyline of the chapters that had been read in preparation for the class; then new vocabulary words were presented by the students; and finally, quotes that the students found especially beautiful or meaningful were discussed. This format provided a dynamic classroom atmosphere, in which the time passed quickly, and the students' interest could be maintained by the great beauty of the literature.

The love story in <u>The English Patient</u> proved to be a supreme motivator for discussion, and, at times, there was such ecstasy in the classroom as the students talked about love. In the novel, the love story is so passionate— *"The heart is an organ of fire."* The students particularly loved this quotation. Some were elated by the love story, but others, possibly because of their traditional value system, were put off by an affair in which the woman in the couple was already married. When we discussed whether the students would have an affair if they were married, I was surprised by the number of young women who said that they would, if they loved another man! Love, the students believed, was paramount, not the traditions of society.

Cold Mountain presented other challenges for the students, because it is written with so many colloquial words from the American South. However, the students found the overall story to be fascinating, particularly the love story and the Civil War background. The novel, Gone with the Wind, is a favorite with Chinese students, so, it was only natural that they would love another Civil War love story. Also, the students had requested that I tell them more about America, and the novel provided a perfect discussion for many American historical, cultural, and environmental or geographical issues.

Bengbu College Redux

The spring semester at Bengbu College was a rebirth in many ways for both the students and myself. Like the spring that was everywhere, it was beautiful—the emerald wheat fields and blossoming fruit trees behind my apartment were beautiful. The students, who during the winter, had gone into seclusion, suddenly were playing badminton, ping-pong, and basketball every (and any) where. Everyone was outside again!

Suddenly, I was rediscovered again as the famous *"laowai"* from America. Everyone wanted to be my friend, and it was impossible to be on campus without people approaching me to talk or just to say hello. I was invited to play ping-pong by many students. My phone rang all the time, as I was called by people whom I did not even know. If I was in the dining hall, both my English students and the students from other departments would join me for meals.

For me, it was nice to have friends on campus. I had met several students from other departments at the college, with whom I developed friendships. One student was interested in poetry, and so, we would get together and recite poetry. Another student would eat dinner with me, but we would also ride bicycles to the nearby mountain. These students were not just interested in learning English, but were rather interested in me as a mentor and teacher. These friendships made me really happy, and I finally felt more at home in China.

Most surprisingly, one day Mr. Wong and Ms. Zhao, my two contact teachers, invited me to go on a long bike ride. We left early one Sunday morning to ride our bikes in the ninety-degree heat to Huaiyuan County, a city near Bengbu. I was in awe of the beauty of the Chinese villages that had appeared along our route in their spring glory: blossoming trees and green fields. We arrived at a big mountain near the Huai River, and climbed to the top of the mountain to visit an ancient temple, which was two thousand years old, and had been founded by the philosopher, Lao Tzu. I was deeply impressed by the age of the temple, which maintained images of various deities such as the god of thunder and rain, and the Jade Emperor. After, we rode into Huaiyuan to have a sumptuous dinner of spicy chicken. By the end of the day, after a ride of ninety kilometers, we rode back to the college, tired yet fulfilled.

I felt myself to be so much more of a part of the campus life—welcomed and happy. Sometimes at night, I would play badminton under the street lights with the students, till I was sweaty with delight. It was warm again, and the Chinese world was blooming with life.

The Red Flag and the Eagle

During my time in China, the relationship between the United States and China had deteriorated for three reasons: Taiwan, the Dalai Lama, and Google. When the United States had sold weapons to Taiwan early in my tenure in China, the Chinese government replied with a strongly worded rebuke to the United States. China regards Taiwan as being a part of the Chinese territory, and the mainland Communist government responds negatively to any actions such as this—especially to weapon sales.

Once, I had an hour-long discussion with the vice president of Bengbu College. He told me that he was a physics professor, and he had gone to an international physics conference. At the gathering, he spoke to an American professor about Taiwan; but the American could not comprehend his position that Taiwan should be part of mainland China. The vice president of the college, who was a man in his late fifties, told me that they were taught from grade school that Taiwan was part of China; he said that he felt hurt that the Westerner could not comprehend this. To the Chinese people, this is not a premise—but a reality. This is a highly charged issue that could potentially lead to a serious conflict between the nations, because the United States supports an independent Taiwan.

The second of the explosive "T's," Tibet, added to the chilly relations between the two countries. The Dalai Lama, the leader of the Tibetan people, was going to pay a visit to Barack Obama at the White House. Although the meeting was not highlighted by the American government, the Dalai Lama did meet with Mr. Obama, which again provoked a strong rebuke from the Chinese government. China regards the Dalai Lama as a separatist, who is trying to reestablish Tibet as a separate country from China. The Chinese believe that Tibet has always been part of the territory of China.

As an expatriate living in China, the increase in the tensions between the two governments made me feel apprehensive over the possibility that a greater conflict might ensue. When you are living in a foreign country, you feel vulnerable to your surroundings, but this is especially so if the country who is employing you is in a dispute with your country. I remembered when the United States was bombing Serbia during the Kosovo conflict, but mistakenly bombed the Chinese embassy, killing some diplomats. In response, there were many demonstrations at the American embassy and at consulates. So, I was praying that things were to going to get better, but unfortunately that was not to be the case.

Then, the Google controversy began, because they claimed hackers backed by the Chinese government had accessed the email accounts of Chinese dissidents living in the United States. The United States government formally requested that the Chinese investigate the matter. Google threatened to leave China and to unblock websites that they had previously consented to block so as to remain in concordance with the regulations of Chinese censorship. The Chinese said that all foreign companies had to obey Chinese law. During this time, I was highly anxious about Google not being available as a search engine, because I feared that my access to American websites would be further curtailed.

Not long thereafter, Google left mainland China by reestablishing its site in Hong Kong, and by unblocking the websites. On the day that Google left the mainland, all of the information from their search engine was suddenly in Chinese and in English. The Communist Chinese government responded quickly by blocking the websites, which they had considered politically sensitive or against Chinese law. It was an impasse of international proportions, which highlights the problems that can potentially arise for corporations doing business in foreign countries.

While in China, I followed the news closely. The American media never portrays anything about China that is not in a pejorative manner, and likewise the same can be said of the Chinese media toward the United States. The people of both countries are always getting a biased viewpoint of the news.

The primary lesson that I had learned from my Chinese students was that there is a collective Chinese mind, which is not just fostered by the government, but which is the substance of Chinese opinion. The American media always portrays the people as somehow being manipulated by the Chinese government. One example of this Chinese mindset was a discussion that I'd had with a Buddhist at the temple near the Bengbu College campus. She emphatically stated that the Dalai Lama was trying to break Tibet away from China. It shocked me that the Dalai Lama was not respected by a Chinese Buddhist, but that he was viewed rather as being a negative force against China. These ideas are not just Communist government propaganda, but are a part of the Chinese public mind.

In many classes, my students and I discussed the cultural differences between the two countries. The histories of the two countries have been brought to form different approaches to life: American individualism and Chinese collectivism. A very wise man once said, "To understand is to forgive." By understanding other cultures we can foster peaceful and complementary policies, rather than reactive policies based on our own country's vision of the world. China is never going to be an individualistic country—there is a collective Han mind, which is the basis for the country. Foreign policies based on confrontation rather than on understanding can only lead to conflict.

After the terrorist attacks on September 11th, 2001, someone asked a great spiritual leader what the response of the United States should be. He responded, "They need to listen." If we are able to listen to what other countries in the world are saying—and, moreover, understand their cultural imperatives—then there can be dialogue rather than confrontation and war. This was the lesson that I learned from my Chinese students.

Green Hats and Dental Floss

Culture is a group of commonly held and shared assumptions in a society, which promotes social functioning and welfare. China, because it has been historically isolated from the world at periods during its history, presents a unique laboratory for the dynamics of intercultural meetings. The Chinese people react strongly to the presence of a foreigner, especially in areas like the Anhui Province where foreigners are rare. Consequently, the Chinese person greets the foreigner with curiosity, astonishment, and with, at times, suspicion. I was the subject of much bemusement whenever in public, where I would be greeted with chuckles, stares, and hellos from all sides. I was told that the foreign teacher before me at Bengbu College complained about these interactions to the college administrators. Psychologically, it is not easy to be the center of attention all of the time!

It was a cold winter day in the classroom, and as usual, I was dressed from head to toe in a coat, gloves, and a hat—a green hat. A male student said to me, "Why are you wearing a green hat? Do you see anyone else here wearing a green hat?" I thought to myself that this was a strange question…"Green hat?" He said, "Yeah, wearing a green hat means something bad—that someone has had sex with your wife." I laughed and said something like, "I like green and that's why I wear a green hat." What was stranger was that it made me think that I did not want to stick out any further than I had done already, so I started wearing my blue hat for a time. I would always joke with this student that I was going to wear my green hat.

Then, when St. Patrick's Day came, I wore my green hat again, not just to celebrate being partly Irish, but because I wanted to shock the Chinese sensibility again and be truly different and foreign. I wore the green hat every day until the weather became warm. I joked with the one student who had brought this green hat belief to me that I was going to come to him in his dreams wearing my green hat. As I walked around the campus wearing my hat, I heard laughter and saw smiles. I was a real *"laowai"* and a cuckhold. The funny thing was that the young men never wore hats even in the coldest weather. So, I really stood out.

One day, I went to see my advisor, Derrick, in his office because I'd had a problem. I told him that I had gone to all of the stores in the area trying to buy dental floss, but that I could not find any. I asked him if he knew where I could purchase some. He looked at me just as though I had asked him where the Martian embassy was! He asked me what dental floss was. I tried to explain to him that it was used by Westerners for dental hygiene, or to clean their teeth after eating. He again looked at me like the Martians had just landed in Bengbu. I then gave it a last try by demonstrating with my hands how you held the piece of string and moved it in between your teeth. His reaction was then as though, now, he were seeing the Martian flying saucers landing in Bengbu. Derrick then typed dental floss into his computer, so as to translate the term into Chinese. When he found it, he was obviously relieved; but he then said that they did not have it in Bengbu. He told me that they might have it in the bigger Chinese cities. It was then that I realized that the Chinese use toothpicks to clean their teeth, not dental floss. I was in a real fix, and so I had to have a friend mail me some dental floss in a care package from America. Fearing that I would run out before the package had arrived, I would reuse the dental floss— yuck!

Another China 'happening' was the day that the flush toilet in my apartment had backed up and would not flush. I knew that I had only needed a common plunger to plunge out the toilet, but I was in China. In China, as in much of Asia, squat toilets are used in bathrooms—a person squats over the porcelain squatting area and defecates; there is no toilet seat or water to flush. I thought to myself, "Do they even have plungers in China?" I called a student friend, and after much explanation as to what a plunger was, he said that there was no plunger in his dormitory. He said that maybe they would have one at the big department store in Bengbu. I then went to the dining hall to have dinner, where I encountered another student who had said that they might have a plunger at the local store. He walked with me to the student shopping area, and asked the clerk in Chinese whether they'd had a plunger. She immediately pointed out a large black plunger, just like one from America. I was overjoyed, and returned to my apartment to unplug my toilet. Ah, the joys of living in a foreign country.

Another very controversial subject for students in China is the innumerable examinations that they have to pass in order to obtain a higher education. It is like jumping hurdles in a track event, where only the best hurdlers get to progress to the next race. When a student in China finishes high school, they must pass an examination if they want to attend a college or a university. Of course, so many students want to go on for a college degree, but I was told by a student that only about thirty percent pass the test with a score that is high enough to permit them to advance towards a higher degree of education. The rest are relegated to the technical schools to learn a trade, or simply just to enter the Chinese workforce.

However, this is just one of the many examinations that students must take during their college years. There is one examination after another—each one a gate in a Mandarin court that either bars or allows advancement towards a closeness with one's own goals in life. Every time a provincial examination was to be held at Bengbu College, the building where the exam was to be held would be cordoned off with yellow tape—just like the type that the police in America use at a murder scene. Murder scene—well, I was to find out that these exams had terminated the educational life of many Chinese college students.

In April of 2010, exams were held at our college to determine which students would be allowed to finish their college coursework and to obtain a bachelor's degree. My student friend, Robert, was among the students to take the test, as were many of the students that I knew. They were all petrified that they would fail and have to get a job. Also, if they failed, they could retake the test in two years. Robert told me that, out of about ninety students taking the test, only forty would be allowed to finish their college undergraduate career. During my stay in China, it was one of the saddest days when Robert called to tell me that he had failed to make the cut-off by eight points: he would not be permitted to go on with his education. In America, I told him, there was always an appeal process, and I told him maybe he could appeal the decision. He said he would try to find out about an appeals process, but when he had contacted the school officials about it, he was warned that he would suffer future repercussions if he had tried to appeal! Robert was going to have to wait two years to retake the examination.

Of all of the complaints that Chinese students made to me—and these were few—the greatest problems in their lives were the examinations. They regarded them as unfair, and not reflective of their educational abilities. They universally believed that there should be a free higher education for all. I too agreed with the students' position that education should be for all, but in China, the examination system has a long history of being the way of determining passage into higher education. It is not likely to change.

There are so many examples of the clash between cultures that I had experienced in China. The one Chinese habit that I had had the most problem with was spitting. The Chinese spit everywhere! I could walk around the campus or on any street in Bengbu City, and see gobs of spit resplendent on the sidewalk. What really offended my Western sensibilities, though, was when people would gather a big hocker in their throats and spit on the dining room floor. Or, several times I was sitting with students eating dinner, and they would spit on the floor next to themselves. Although this is very acceptable behavior in China, it is the height of barbarism in the Western world. To my mind, spitting on the floor in the dining hall was despicable.

It also really disturbed me greatly, when Chinese men tried to spit up pieces of their respiratory system in the morning, while clearing out their throats in order to purge all mucous from their systems. The sound is so loud and offensive to Western ears—what a wakeup call!

I had too often reflected about the way Chinese children urinate and defecate on public streets through a slit in their trousers. Yes, little Chinese children's clothing is designed with a slit in the backside so they can squat on the street and do their business. Although this is the most innocent activity in the world, to my Western mind, it seemed unhygienic to have urine and feces on the sidewalk. It was just one of those cultural differences that befuddled and baffled my mind.

Another really offensive thing for me in China was the unconcern for pedestrian safety, and how traffic, specifically taxis and buses, would never stop and just run you down if you were in the way. I felt as though I had to have eyes on not only the back of my head, but ones that would be positioned in such a way they could look in all directions for traffic, like the eyes of a hyper-caffeinated lizard. In some foreign countries, traffic can be disturbing, and have no apparent methodology except to force everything to continue to go forward, but in China the ante was upped considerably by the speed of the moving traffic. People drive as fast as they can, even in crowded pedestrian areas. Every day, I saw cars or motorcycles going sixty miles an hour through the university district, as hordes of students were crossing the street.

The students told me stories about how in China motorists had even killed people, but they were able through family influence and money to buy their way out of severe punishment. There was one famous case involving a drunken driver who had killed several people, but who was able to avoid the death penalty by paying a fortune to the courts. Once, I asked my Chinese friend why the police didn't give these speeders a ticket. She said, "Oh, they would just make an arrangement with the police." I thought to myself, "What a system of justice!"

Then, the group of speeders that I disliked the most were the electric motorcycle owners. You could never hear them as they approached when you were walking or riding a bike, because these vehicles are completely silent. It was a daily occurrence for me to be frightened as one of these would zip inches away from my legs, as I was walking through campus. Yes, vehicles would just appear out of nowhere on campus, riding on the sidewalks and everywhere. I always had to be on alert for them, and had never trusted these motorists not to aim for my *"laowai"* legs.

Once, I was walking with a student after class, when she looked at me and told me that I opened my mouth too wide when eating with my chopsticks. I was surprised by this unexpected comment, but I was always being watched wherever I was on campus. I didn't realize that I was doing something wrong according to Chinese sensibilities. My mouth was probably getting too close to my big American nose! It was a strange world that I was living in while staying on campus.

Every morning, when it was a sunny day, all the Chinese students and teachers would hang their bed quilts over the fences, exercise equipment, and out of their dormitory windows to dry. I loved to see the patchwork quilt of so many colors and designs festooning the campus. One day, a student had asked me why I didn't put my quilt out to dry. I looked at him and said that, "I had never thought about it." It was something we never did in America. He looked at me with a look that was like he was unable to process what I had just said. I thought he was trying to figure out why he hung his quilt out. It was as if my lack of culture was like a piece of meat sticking in his teeth.

When the Spring Festival came that year, the students had all asked me where I was going to spend my holiday, and whether I was going to travel back to America. I told him that I couldn't because it would cost too much money. When I told them that I was going to stay in Jiuhuashan by myself for three weeks, they looked at me with a quizzical expression. It was as if they were saying, "Why would anyone spend the Spring Festival by themselves?" During the Spring Festival, it is paramount for the Chinese people to be with their families. They could not understand my American individualistic value of being able to spend the time alone, and to enjoy by myself.

Once, I was eating lunch in a restaurant in Bengbu, while sitting in front of a large glass picture window. A young woman was walking by the window, and when she saw me, she screeched to a halt, stood, and stared at me in the window. She could not believe what she was seeing—a foreigner before her eyes. I was deeply impressed by this, and reflected how just my very presence was an alien intrusion into the Chinese consciousness.

Another example of this was when I would eat my meals in the hotel restaurant in Jiuhuashan. When food would be delivered to my table by the waitress, every Chinese person around me would turn their heads to see what I was eating. One time, people actually got up from their tables in front of me, walked over to my table, and looked to see what I was eating. I was just such an unusual specimen to Chinese eyes, and, of course, I did not know how or what to eat!

Whether it was green hats or dental floss, living in China was always a clash of cultures...particularly for me, because I would flaunt my American ways sometimes just to show people that—yes, there is another way to live and to act!

What Color Is the Sky?

When I had first come to China, a Chinese teacher told me about an examination question that she had asked her students. The question was: "What color is the sky?" She told me that the students had unanimously written the answer: "white." I laughed uncontrollably when she had said this. I thought that this was hysterically funny, as did the Chinese teacher. Of course, there are some days when the Chinese sky is blue, but these days are rare indeed. In fact, the sky is most usually white. After my first visits to China, I would always reflect about this phenomenon and wonder if it was just the pollution. My inner belief was that it probably was due to the ever-present pollution.

Over the months, and the more I lived in China, though, when I thought about the question—"What color is the sky?"—I came to believe that maybe the Chinese students were right. The sky really is white in China. Their answer was not just some laughable supposition on their part, but rather a statement of the reality of their short lives in comparison to those who had lived into their mature or elderly years. Most of my students were only eighteen years old, and probably during their lives, the sky has been only white. They have only lived during the rapid development of the Chinese economy with its concomitant pollution.

My entire experience in China had shown me that what we perceive as reality is filtered by our culture, by our education, and for most humans, by our senses. It was clear to me that cultures are just common assumptions that groups of people have come to practice, and in the case of China, have been practiced for thousands of years. For a Chinese person, to see someone wearing a green hat was so improbable as to be hysterical. Then, someone from the foreign culture appeared in their midst with his big nose wearing a green hat. I realized that the shock of my green hat and average Western nose had made them think about why they had believed the things that they believed. And, at the same time for me, I had to look at why I was so offended by a baby urinating in the street. The meeting of cultures is an awakening to the fact that what we perceive as reality may be only that: a perception, an assumption. Only when confronted by another who comes from outside of the cultural system can there even be a reflection about why we behave the way we do in our everyday lives.

Simultaneously, I came to realize by living in a foreign culture, that everything we perceive as real is just a conditional viewpoint based on our culture, our education, and our very limited sensory input. Is the sky really blue? I know that, at least where I lived in China, it is not. I realized that people can only understand the world by staying open to the possibility of other realities, and of other cultures, like China's—that are much, much older, and, if I may say, wiser than our own. I know with all certainty that I had only perceived a very small fraction of the reality of Chinese life and culture. I did not speak the language. My students were the lens with which I was able to glimpse a small, very limited view of Chinese life. I was like the proverbial blind men trying to describe the elephant—one said that it was like a pillar as he grasped the leg; one said it was like a fan as he touched the ear; and the other said that it was definitely like a snake as he held onto the trunk. I'm sure that I've only touched a toenail of the whole "elephant" that I've tried in these pages to describe. At the same time, I hope and pray, that I was able to give them some sense of what it is like to be an American, or to see through their own 'laowai' eyes as an American, somewhat or perhaps more than previously.

It is so difficult to see our own cultures, because it is with our culture that we often see or perceive what may be before us at any time, and just as we forget about the glasses that might sit on the bridges of our noses, the viewpoints that we have become invisible thereby. However, if we do come into contact with another viewpoint—a culture other than our own—by working in a "foreign" capacity as a teacher, say, our own viewpoint can become apparent to us, and the glasses that we had known so to be such familiar lenses can slip from the bridge of our nose. We become open to the unknowable nature of Reality, and to the wonderment of what all of us are trying to learn in any way that we might go at it. Lenses, after all, do distort as well as reveal. And sometimes, when we can let them go, things become clearer...

There is a famous saying of the Prophet Muhammad, *"Follow wisdom even unto China."* Like Diogenes, I had traveled along my own Silk Road, with my lighted lantern into the Chinese agora of Bengbu College. I too was looking for something—maybe like Diogenes, a real human being, or perhaps, myself. Certainly I was looking for wisdom in the Chinese sky. What I found were my students, the true angels of this earth. They told me the sky is really white, and I believe them.

EPILOGUE

Kites

A student had told me about an old Chinese allegory. He said that, even when a kite is flying high in the sky, it is still attached by string to the flyer of the kite. He said that the Chinese believed that kites are like children, and no matter how high they may fly or how far they may go, they are always attached to their mother's hands.   I realized that China and America are like children, and we are attached to the same mother's hand, Mother Earth's. We are children of the same mother who loves us dearly. A great teacher once said, *"The highest form of love is respect."* When America and China learn to respect each other, and realize that we are children of the same mother; then, like kites, we will fly so high together, and create a beautiful, peaceful earth.

Bengbu College

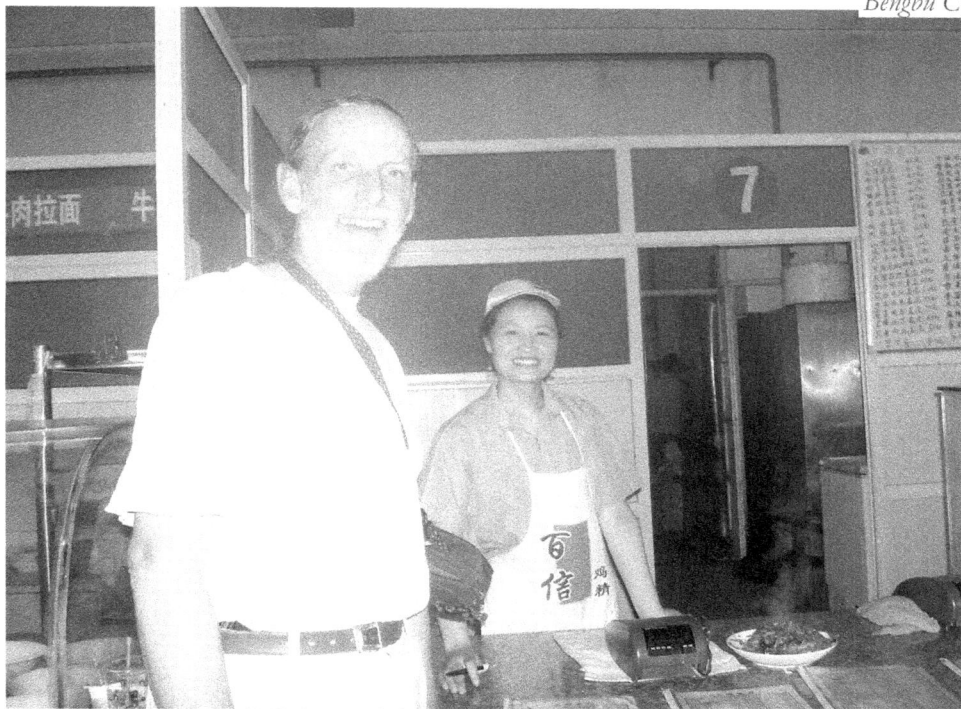

"There Is No Sandwich," *Cafeteria of Bengbu College*

South Village, Bengbu College

"Diogenes of Sinope"

Bengbu College Dormitories

Shanghai--The Bund, June, 2010

Bengbu Buddhist Temple

www.ingramcontent.com/pod-product-compliance
Lightning Source LLC
Chambersburg PA
CBHW052008090426
42741CB00008B/1606